GRAYSHOTT

from Then to Now

GRAYSHOTT
From Then to Now

The Growth of an English Village

John P. Hill

Grayshott – from Then to Now

First published 2019

Published by Noyant Publications, Grayshott GU26 6TN

Typeset by John Owen Smith

ISBN 978-0-9928472-1-0

Printed by KDP

A WORD FROM ...

Mr Phil Bates

It is a great honour and pleasure for me to write a foreword for "Grayshott, from Then to Now".

This book is a charming mixture of local history and village life; in fact it covers the history of Grayshott over the best part of a thousand years, from very early to modern times.

John Hill's book illustrates extremely well and concisely how the growth and life of a community are inseparable, and that a stable community can survive almost anything but indifference.

Having lived in Grayshott for over fifty years I found, after reading "Grayshott, from Then to Now", that I came away with a sense of pride for our village. From start to finish I was fascinated with its history, and the detail of so much that has happened, which this book has captured so well, and accurately. I am confident that all those who are fortunate enough to read the book will feel likewise.

In my opinion, Grayshott village is in much need of an up-to-date book explaining its whole history, with full colour, which John has succeeded in writing; a work of which other villages will surely be envious.

Phil Bates, 2019

CONTENTS

INTRODUCTION

It is said that, in order to understand the present, we need to appreciate our past. This is certainly relevant in the context of the development and growth of Grayshott, from its very early beginnings to the vibrant community that it has become today. The origins of the village have influenced what it is today, and we cannot understand where we are now without examining how we got here.

The whole of Grayshott covers some 901 acres, is about 650 feet above sea level, the whole area standing on the Hampshire/Surrey border to the north and east. The Parish is in a region of great scenic beauty, surrounded on three sides by woodland, wooded valleys and common. The whole area is threaded with footpaths and within minutes from the village centre it is possible to be deep in pleasant rolling countryside.

From its very early beginnings, as a nearby rural hamlet, to that of a modern thriving community, the development of Grayshott is the story of a village which has grown not only through changes in English society over the decades, but also because of the hard work and generosity that was bestowed by certain families and individuals at the time, all playing a major part in the growth of the village.

In the pages that follow, we go on a journey, travelling in time from the Norman Conquest to the present day. We see the influences that were in play at the time, including the coming of the railways as well as two world wars which did much to shape the society in which we live today.

I hope you enjoy the journey.

CHAPTER ONE

BEGINNINGS

Until the middle part of the 19th century, during the reign of Queen Victoria, Grayshott, as a village and as a community, simply did not exist as we know it today.

There was no Headley Road, no Crossways Road, no shops, pub, and only a handful of dwellings. Neither St. Luke's nor St. Joseph's Churches had yet been built, and the nearest road of note was the Portsmouth Road, which ran just over a mile away, to the east, and served to link London with the coastal areas of Portsmouth.

There were to be found the odd small farm holdings and rough cottages, however, in such places as Stoney Bottom and Whitmore Vale, in isolated spots where the low-lying valleys ran up in a general north east direction to meet the more elevated land at Hindhead. The higher ground in this area was in places bare and virtually waterless. It was in these surroundings that the scant population eked out a living as best could be achieved.

In general terms, however, a large part of the area of land we now call the village of Grayshott was simply sparse open waste land, with poor soil and rough vegetation consisting mainly of gorse, heather, pine and the like.

It was neither good arable nor grazing land, but little more than mean scrubby countryside. And it had a reputation for lawlessness, with robbers and thieves frequenting the area, with fugitives from justice to be found, known as "runagates". Not an encouraging place in which to live or raise a family.

Having said thus, we can see that the tentacles of history do in fact take Grayshott back many centuries in time, with records to be found as early as the 12th century and before. The reason for this apparent discrepancy is that there was an earlier, and long established settlement of that name, not where the village is today, but about a mile to the west of it, in the neighbourhood and mainly to the north west of where we now find Grayshott Hall, along the Headley Road. This was a small, agricultural-based, hamlet community located in what was then the ancient Parish of Headley, a Domesday parish which, before the Norman Conquest in 1066, was part of the estates in the ownership of Earl Godwin of Wessex.

Earl Godwin (died April 1053) was one of the most powerful earls in England under the Danish king Cnut and his successors and had extensive estates throughout the south of England and beyond. He was the father of King Harold and also of Edith of Wessex, who became the wife of Edward the Confessor.

Godwin, Earl of Essex 1001–1053

King Stephen 1095–1154

After the Norman Conquest, the area changed hands many times over the years. At the time of "The Great Survey" known as the Domesday Book (1085) it was in the ownership of Eustace, Count of Boulogne. His own son, also named Eustace, married Mary of Scotland, following which their own daughter Matilda was married to King Stephen (1135 to 1154).

Later, King Stephen transferred all the royal manor lands to his brother Henry of Blois, who was also the Bishop of Winchester at the time. Thereafter it stayed in the ownership of the Bishopric of Winchester for several centuries .

The first time we come across the name in a recognisable form was in 1185, when "Gravuesseta" was referred to in the "Pipe Rolls". These hand-written documents were the financial records of the Crown, which contained such details as land rents, feudal taxes and offerings for the king's favour, and which were produced each year. A few years later, in 1200, we come across reference to "Graveschete" in the "Episcopal Registers", which were maintained by the scribes of the Church, and which contained details of all properties owned by the diocese, together with changes to parishes, appointments and the like.

Towards the original settlement, Grayshott Spa in the foreground

Life in the old farming community of Grayshott would not have been easy. The land was of relatively poor soil and drainage, with a cool micro-climate, and the living was generally sparse. Certain parts could be used for arable and pasture, the crops being mostly oats and rye, and livestock would also have been grazed on the surrounding common land. Each of the farms would have had a small number of sheep, pigs and cattle. The adjoining woodland areas would have been used for such activities as coppicing, the right to take turf, firewood, bracken and the woodland grazing of animals where possible.

The struggle to survive was not made easy by the recurring threats of famine, crop failure, disease and political strife, which were a common factor of life throughout the country. One such event occurred in the fourteenth century, and was known as the Black Death. There is no direct evidence that the Grayshott hamlet was affected, but it would be impossible to believe that it escaped the scourge, and the privations that resulted.

The Black Death, also known as the Great Plague, was without a doubt the most devastating pandemic in the whole of human history. Moving out from the plains of Central Asia, it raged relentlessly across the whole of Europe from around 1346 to 1353.

The effect was badly felt throughout the country, where whole communities were decimated. Death and suffering at the time was widespread, and there were simply no effective remedies available to counter its spread. With farming communities, the main effect of the plague was that, over a period of a few years, there grew a shortage of labour to manage the land, which meant that the growing of crops suffered, as did the manpower available to tend the herds of animals. As the plague wiped out whole families, in the South East and elsewhere it left about half of the houses in the area derelict as a result of depopulation.

It took many years and decades for the farming communities of Britain to recover from the scourge of the Plague. Life for the small farmer was hard at the best of times, where crop failures or animal sickness was never far away and could lead to famine for the family. However, as time progressed, the local farming community in the old Grayshott struggled and managed to rebuild and survive .

Indeed, by the Tudor times (the period between 1485 and 1603, which coincides with the dynasty of the House of Tudor in England), we know of a number of specific farm areas in the hamlet, namely Bulls (occupied by William Graveshott junior), Kings (William Langford), Barneland (John Warner), Highe Graveshott (Richard Chitty), Grasseat (Robert Luckin), Home House (John Warner) and Yalcroft & Bryghtnesse (Richard Gill). Life on the farms was tough in those days, but at least it secured a living for the families there.

In 1553 the area was called Graveshotte and, in the years that followed, the name changed to its current spelling probably around the 18th century. A detailed survey of the area made in the reign of King Edward VI (1547–53) used the similar name Graveshot and describes an area of "waste".

The suffix "shott" in local names generally referred to springs flowing from the sandstone rock strata, this being one of several possible derivations.

The Grayshott farmers and other occupiers of the land were tenants of the manor of Sutton, in the ownership of the Bishop of Winchester, as we have seen. What occurred over the years and the decades that followed was that this large land holding became gradually subdivided, as various parts of the estate were sold off into new ownerships. We know that one of those sub divisions occurred when a part of the Parish of Headley, including the area of the original Graveshotte, came into the ownership of the then Manor of Wishanger in the latter part of the eighteenth century.

The Manor of Wishanger, at the time, extended all the way from Frensham Great Pond on its Western border to Hindhead Common to its East, and included parts of Frensham, Churt, Headley and Ludshott as we know it today.

Although they were only tenants of the land, the freehold of which was owned by the Manor, the farmers and other occupiers had a number of important customary rights, which were recognised by law, and which enabled them to benefit to a certain extent from whatever fruits and benefits the land had to offer.

For example, the "Register of Fines" of the earlier Manor of Sutton stated that:

> "We present the tenants of Headley to have the right to cut turf in the Common to burn in their houses and not elsewhere". And,
>
> "We present that the coppeyholders in the tything of Heathley may cut what turff they will burn in their houses, but not to burn on the Common or on their enclosed lands for if they do so they shale pay two pounds and ten shillings to the Lord of the Manor and fifty shillings to the informer. We present that no coppeyholders in the same tything shall cut any firz or heath to burn lime to carry out of the tything upon the forfeit of ten shillings to the Lord of the Manor and ten shillings to the informer".

In the same vein, it was stated in a note in the 18th century that:

> "The copyholders under the Bishop have an immemorial Right of cutting whatever shrubwood they have occasion for in Whitmore Bottom and also in the Bottom near Wakeners Wells ponds for making outside fences but no other".

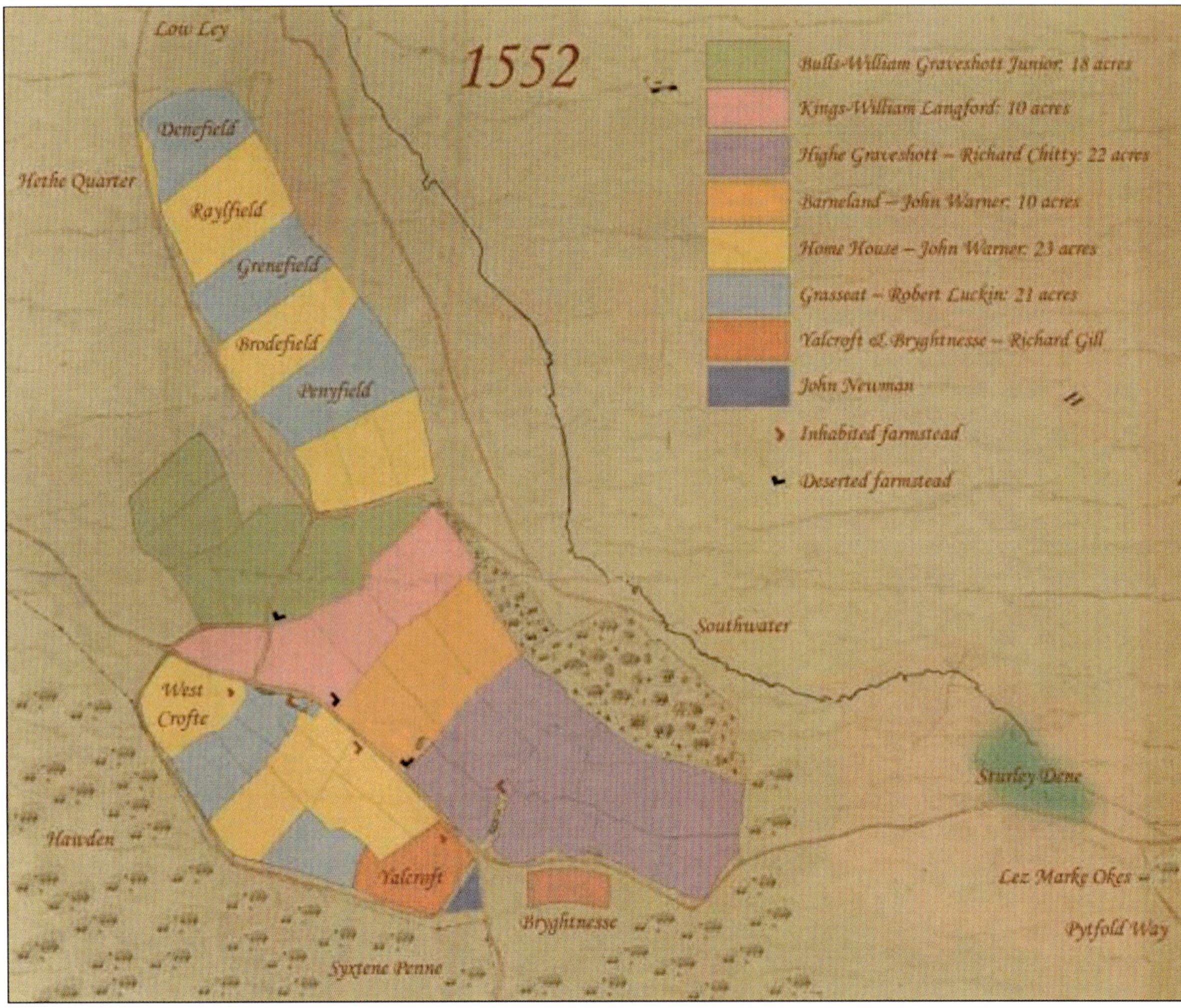

The old Grayshott fields, 1552

Waggoners Wells, a modern scene

The area that we now know as Waggoners Wells, off the Headley Road, was at that time called Wakeners Wells, created at the time by the Hooke family, who were Lords of the Manor of neighbouring Bramshott. A local stream, being one of the headwaters of the River Wey, was first dammed in the early 17th century in order to form the three ponds as we know them today.

It is suggested that these stretches of water were originally intended to be used as "hammer ponds" in the area where, due to the combination of iron in the soil plus timber for charcoal and water power, many iron furnaces were constructed. These iron furnaces were at one time a common feature of the area, as part of the extensive iron industry which stretched across the whole region as far as Sussex, but which died out gradually in the south of England with the denuding of the woods which supplied the charcoal for the furnaces, which in turn coincided with the development of smelting by coal and coke.

The frequent occurrence of the word "hammer" in the locality (the word is found locally to this day) suggests the extent of an industry which is thought to have dated from as far back as the period of the Roman occupation.

After this industrial era, it is thought that the lakes were converted into fish ponds by the then Lord of the Manor at the time, for the sole purposes of recreation. To a certain extent, however this is conjecture, as there is no clear historic evidence either way.

Today, close by the ford that leads to the first of the ponds, there is a memorial stone to Sir Robert Hunter (1844–1913). He was one of the driving forces (together with Octavia Hill and Hardwicke Rawnsley) behind the creation of the National Trust, which came into being in January 1895, conceived as a "not for profit" association with the main object of protecting open spaces as well as a variety of threatened buildings.

The stone was erected, after his death, in 1919, and interestingly the inscription uses the spelling "Waggeners" in its description of the site. The Trust now owns the ponds and the surrounding areas, which are maintained as a valuable leisure facility, a popular place to walk and enjoy the countryside.

After several changes of ownership, all of the lands which included the old Grayshott (also called Greyshott and Greyshotte) at the time passed into the hands of the Speed family towards the end of the 18th century (John Speed being described as "A Doctor of Physick of Southampton"). After several changes of ownership, both within the family and as a result of marriage, in 1797 the Wishanger estate was sold to one Sir Thomas Miller of Froyle for £4,500, a very considerable sum in those days.

Sir Thomas was a wealthy landowner, and also an English politician, being Member of Parliament for Lewes from 1774 to 1778 and then representing Portsmouth from the years 1806 to 1816. The estate remained in the Miller family until 1868, when it was sold to John Rouse Phillips, who was believed to be a descendant of the Philips brewery family. It is believed that it was Phillips who changed the name of what was then described as Grayshott Hall Farm to that of Grayshott Hall. On his death in 1884 it was sold to a certain Mr Joseph Whitaker "of Yorkshire and Palermo" for the stated sum of £50,954.

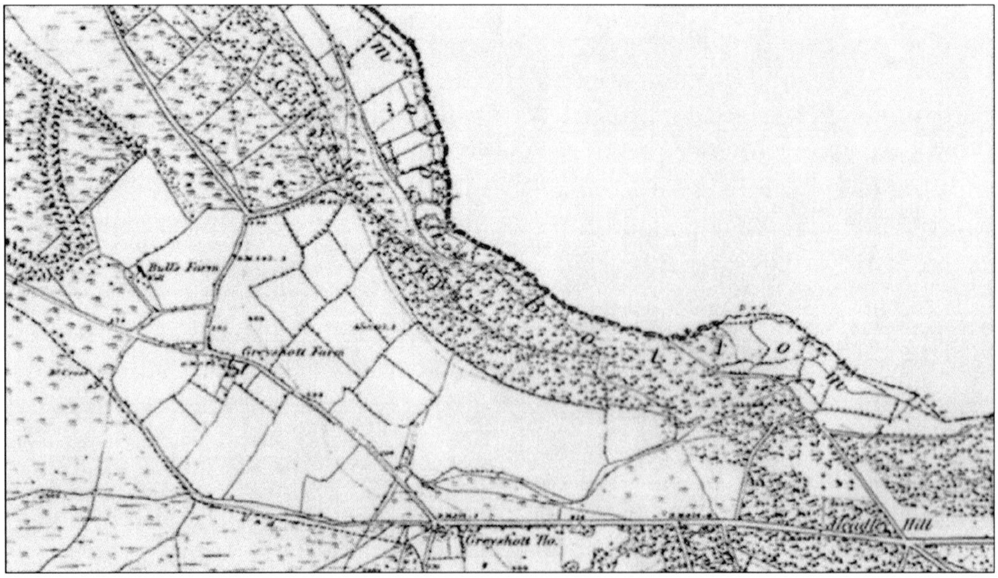

Grayshott in 1869

Grayshott early 1800s

The Whitakers were a wealthy 19th century family hailing originally from an estate, Hesley Hall, in Tickhill, West Yorkshire. As well as their interests in Britain, the Whitakers also had extensive business concerns in Palermo in Sicily, where, amongst other things, they were instrumental in the development of a successful fortified wine industry in Marsala, leading to a large export trade in the world-famous Marsala wine. Several members of the Whitaker family had in fact moved to Sicily permanently, and became a major economic and cultural influence in Italian society during the nineteenth century.

Joseph Whitaker himself owned the Grayshott estate for just a short time, and, following his sudden death a year later in Palermo, the land passed to his son, Mr Alexander Ingham Whitaker. He was born in September 1857, and later educated at Harrow School and Trinity College, Cambridge.

Joseph Whitaker
1802–1884

Thus begun a long period when the Whitaker family was to become well known in the Grayshott area, and influential in the development of the village.

The middle years of the reign of Queen Victoria saw wide ranging and fundamental changes in the social fabric of the whole of Great Britain. The technology of the Industrial Revolution had a massive impact on the whole society, and inventions not only helped to create new industries and manufacturing processes but also resulted in a growing need for employed labour, specifically in the towns and cities.

The population of England almost doubled from 16.8 million in 1851 to 30.5 million in 1901, and at the same time there was a rapid improvement in communications generally. Stage coaches, steamships and, most notably, the railways all speeded up the movement of people, goods and ideas with it. Trains opened up leisure destinations, and encouraged people to travel from the cities to explore the surrounding areas.

These, and other changes were to have a profound effect on the development of Grayshott, and the community that it was to become in the decades that followed. These changes were to see the birth and development of the village as we know it today.

CHAPTER TWO

GRAYSHOTT – THE EARLY YEARS

From the 1840s onwards, a number of forces and influences were at work which, over the years, gave birth to the village of Grayshott as we know it today. These were to see a change in the nature and character of the village, from a hamlet collection of a small number of farm-related buildings spreading only to about 130 acres near the present location of Hammer Lane, to the thriving community as we know and recognise today, in its permanent location closer to Hindhead and Haslemere, on the Surrey border.

The initial influence was The Headley Enclosure Award of 1849, which gave rise to the enclosure of land in and around Headley (which included Grayshott, at the time, being part of the same Parish).

The Inclosure Acts (or "Enclosure" in modern spelling) were a number of Acts of Parliament which gave rise to the enclosure of certain common lands and open fields, creating legal property rights over land that was previously regarded as being used in common for everyone.

Prior to the enclosures in England, a portion of the land was categorised as "common". This was under the control of the Lord of the Manor, but a number of rights on the land, such as the right to pasture, were held by neighbouring properties or, if it was not otherwise used, it was often cultivated by landless peasants.

In addition, some areas of land were described as "waste", ie little or no value. These were often in awkward locations, like cliff edges or inconveniently shaped borders of land. As such, they were not officially used by anyone, and thus were often left to be cultivated by subsistence farmers as best they could.

The remainder of the land was organised into strips, called the open field system, with each tenant possessing a number of strips. These could be used for grazing and crop rotation, but still owned by the Lord of the Manor. The open field system was administered by the manorial courts, which exercised some form of collective control.

In the quest for more efficient farming techniques, landowners looked for improved ways of utilising the land in search for better financial returns. With the rise of new agricultural knowledge and technology in the 18th and 19th centuries, Inclosure Acts became more common-place. By gaining legal control of the land, landlords were encouraged to utilise innovations in methods of crop production, thus increasing both productivity and resulting profits. A side effect of this was, however, that the tenants were often displaced. As a result, many left the countryside to find work in the towns and cities. This in turn contributed to the many social problems that arose out of the Industrial Revolution, when former country tenants and their families and descendants became workers in industrial factories, living far away from their roots.

A number of Inclosure Acts had been passed sporadically since as far back as the 12th Century, which affected various parts of the country at the time. Aside from this, however, the main driving force was the changing world resulting from the Industrial Revolution, with the need and the drive for more efficient farming. This, in turn, gave rise to many more such Acts in the 19th Century.

The Act that gave rise to the changes in our area was the Headley Award in the late 1840s, which had a great influence in the shaping of society in this part of Hampshire.

The proposal for enclosure was in respect of 1,667 acres described partly as being of "waste of manor" of Headley Common and other lands in the Parish, which included the areas of land which now comprise the present village. In the introduction to the legislation, the Inclosure Commissioners reported that:

> "We consider this proposed enclosure expedient, on the ground that, by draining and cultivation, a considerable portion of the land may be rendered very productive, and useful employment, of which the labouring population stand in need, afforded to them".

The result of the passing of the Act of 1849 was that areas of land came up for sale for the very first time, at a variable price of around £7 per acre, and by this means the land could be passed into private ownership. This resulted in the development of land taking place in the area over the years and decades that followed.

A sale notice which appeared in the London press, dating from the middle of the nineteenth century, for example, states:

> "Instructions from the Inclosure Commissioners, Headley Common Inclosure, 9th June 1851. Freehold land which with a small expenditure would become highly productive and remunerative…it has romantic views from many parts".

Also: "75 acres situate near Grayshott sold for £137. I should say this is a great Bargain tho' the situation is adjoining a nest of rather rough customers called The Hindhead Gang".

By 1859, the process of enclosing the land, where permitted, was complete. The records show that among the people who took advantage of this were:

Henry Fullick, who paid £4.19.0 for an acre or so in Stoney Bottom.
William Lawrence, who paid £130 for about 20 acres in Whitmore Bottom.

James Baker of Frensham Hall, who paid £140 for some 80 acres.
Charles Andrews of Farnham, who paid £220 for about 32 acres.

Not all the land was sold off into private ownership, however, as certain defined areas were retained for public use and enjoyment, such as allotments, recreation grounds, roads and public footpaths. But the general effect of the enclosures was that the greater part of the land now became available to develop, build houses and shops. The resulting development, over the years, led to an inevitable increase in the population as more and more people took advantage of the opportunities that the legislation presented.

Railway travel in the 1840s

At about the same time as this was happening, great changes were also occurring throughout the whole of the country as a result of an explosion in the extent of the railway network.

From the 1830s onwards, the construction of hundreds of miles of track meant that the railway network had been extending from London and other major cities to all compass points of the kingdom. In the south of England, the network stretched inexorably into Surrey, Hampshire, and other home counties and beyond, reaching Woking in 1838 and Guildford in 1845. A section of railway between Godalming and Havant was built for the Portsmouth Railway Company by the contractor Thomas Brassey, and the line was opened in December 1858.

Haslemere Station was opened in January 1859, with the station booking hall being constructed in the Tudor-revival style, which was popular at the time. There was great popular fanfare at the opening – it meant that Haslemere and its surrounding areas no longer existed in remoteness; the town and outside, from now on, became accessible and inviting to the world in general.

Pleasing heathland in the bracing air

From this point onwards, the reputation of this part of Surrey and Hampshire began to change. The position of Hindhead, being several hundred feet above sea level, with its air quality declared by Professor John Tyndall to be "as pure as that in the Swiss Alps" soon brought a massed influx of visitors and residents from the 1860s onwards.

Professor Tyndall (1820–1893) was an eminent Victorian physicist, who helped to bring popularity to the area. He built "Hindhead House", just to the south of the Devil's Punchbowl, in 1883 and lived there with his wife Louisa until his early death in 1893. A famous Victorian of his age, his wide-ranging studies included the movement of glaciers, the acoustic properties of air and the radiant properties of heat. He was famous for expounding the theories of Charles Darwin, and was a favourite of the famous scientist Michael Faraday.

He was also a noted mountaineer and did much exploring and climbing in the Swiss Alps, which led him to compare the local air of Hindhead favourably with those found on his continental travels.

His promotion of the Hindhead area, however, did him no favours, and he began to take exception to the growing proliferation of houses around his own. He bought up as much neighbouring land that he could and, when this was not enough, he erected huge screens of larch poles covered in heather, some forty feet in height, around his property. This did not endear him to his friends or neighbours, and the screens were to outlive him after his death.

Professor John Tyndall 1820–1893

Tragically, he met with an untimely end. As he grew older, he suffered from insomnia and bad digestion, and one night in 1893 Louisa, intending to give him his night-time drink of magnesia, sadly gave him an overdose of chloral nitrate instead. He died in his wife's arms, gasping "Darling, you have killed your John".

He was buried in St Bartholomew's churchyard, under a great mound of Hindhead heather, but otherwise an unmarked grave, and today he is all but a forgotten figure. Hindhead House is still there today, and is now a house in multiple occupation. In the 1940s an estate was built in the grounds of the House's gardens, and is known as Tyndalls.

With the Devil's Punchbowl and the wide-open spaces giving rise to the epithet of "Little Switzerland", the area quickly gained a reputation for the beauty of the natural features of the countryside. The area was seen as a healthy place in which to live and visit, away from the crowded, noisy industrial and commercial capital of London, from which it was now possible to escape with a train journey of just over an hour.

The Guide books and Brochures at the time spoke of the beautiful natural features of the area, including the Devil's Punchbowl, Waggoners Wells, Hindhead Common and Frensham Ponds amongst others.

The author Thomas Wright in his 1898 book "Hindhead or The English Switzerland" stated that "The air at Hind Head is very clear and, like Selborne, the spot is a veritable Anathoth. Persons living so far above the sea level feel a buoyancy and elasticity unknown to the dwellers in the sober plains. They are indeed a happy race who inhabit Hind Head, inhale its sweet, pure, fine air, and sniff the aroma of its odoriferous pines".

Gradually the local population increased over the years, encouraged by the arrival of such famous persons as Professor Tyndall, the author and poet Alfred (later Lord) Tennyson, the eminent lawyer and jurist Sir Frederick Pollock, and, later, the famous writers George Bernard Shaw and Arthur Conan Doyle. And as more people arrived, both to live in the area as well as to visit, there was a drive to service their needs. Not only to build and then maintain the new houses, but also to supply and provision the occupants and visitors with the goods and services that were required.

In the 1870s, Mr Henry Robinson opened his small shop, the first in the area, just outside the present village, along the Headley Road opposite School Road, and it was also the first shop to receive postal deliveries.

A few years later, on September 22nd 1879, a milestone was reached in the development of the village when an auction of land in Grayshott was held by Henry J E Brake, Auctioneer and Surveyor of Farnborough, at the White Horse Hotel in Haslemere. The land in question comprised almost all of what we now regard as the centre of Grayshott village, the area being bounded by Headley Road, Hill Road, Crossways Road, and Stoney Bottom.

The auction divided the plots into neat strips of freehold land, each having a frontage of roughly twenty feet to the road, to be bought individually or as several lots. The large plan that accompanied the auction showed that several of the plots in Grayshott were in fact already owned by residents, who had previously opened their own shops. However, the auction does mark a significant milestone in the development of the village, in that it laid out the framework for what was to rapidly to become the commercial and social hub of the area in the years to come.

It was at this auction that Henry Robinson bought his three plots in Crossways Road, paying £19.10.0 in total for Plots 66,67 & 68, with a deposit of £2 put down on the day. This led to the building of his new shop, in what was then known as "Upper Grayshott". This was initially a general store, selling many items in demand by villagers of all ages. Later, in 1887, the shop became the first full post office in the village, designated as a sub-office of Petersfield.

In 1890, there appeared an announcement in a local paper stating that:

> "telegrams are now received for transmission at the Grayshott Post Office. By residents at Hindhead and vicinity this is much appreciated."

Unfortunately, Henry's tenure as postmaster did not last long, as he was sacked in 1892, allegedly due to the misbehaviour of his children Peter and Ruth on the Telegraph system.

Particulars and Conditions of Sale

OF

288 PLOTS OF VALUABLE

FREEHOLD BUILDING LAND,

To be Sold by Auction, by

HENRY J. E. BRAKE,

At the "White Horse" Hotel,

HASLEMERE, SURREY,

On MONDAY, September 22nd, 1879,

AT 1 FOR 2 O'CLOCK IN THE AFTERNOON.

The property is situate in the parish of Headley, Hants, on the road from Headley to Godalming, on the Portsmouth road, near to the "Royal Huts" Hotel, and within easy distance of the Haslemere Railway Station on the South Western Main Line, and 41 miles from the Metropolis.

The neighbourhood is one of the healthiest and most salubrious in England, in the midst of the most beautiful varied and extensive scenery—the Selborne and Marley Hills, Hindhead and Blackdown, being within view.

There are many capital Sites for the erection of high-class properties, and at a very moderate cost be able to form immediately secluded and shady walks a desirable feature in the pleasure grounds of a country residence; and the retired man of business wishing to secure select Sites for a residence would do well to inspect this property.

The whole estate slopes gradually to the south, and the air, laden as it is with the perfume of the Heather and Pine, is well known as the finest in England. It is about 600 feet above the level of the sea.

Will be offered in Lots of from 20 feet frontages, by depths of 200 feet; also in plots of from 1 acre to 5 acres in extent, well adapted for Poultry or Cottage Farms.

May be paid for by a deposit of 10 per cent. and the balance (if desired) by monthly instalments of 2s. for each £10 of the purchase-money.

HENRY J. E. BRAKE,
Auctioneer and Estate Agent,
Lynchford House, Farnborough, Hants.

Plans and Particulars may be obtained at the "White Horse" Hotel, Haslemere; the "Royal Huts" Hotel, Hindhead; "Churchward's" Hotel, Aldershot; of W. E. Foster, Esq., Solicitor, Aldershot; or of the Auctioneer.

Auction particulars September 1879

MEMORANDUM.

I Henry Robinson
of Mount Cottage Headley Green do hereby acknowledge that I have this day purchased Lots 66, 67 & 68 of the property within described, for the sum of £ 19. 10. 0, and have paid to the Auctioneer the sum of £ ~~19. 10. 0~~ 2. 0. 0 as a deposit and in part payment of the purchase-money. And I hereby agree to pay the balance thereof, and in all other respects on my part to fulfil and abide by the within Conditions of Sale, with the alterations (if any) made therein by the Auctioneer at the time of sale.

Dated this 22 day of Sep. 1879

Purchase Money ... ... £ 19. 10. 0
Deposit ... ... £ 2. 0. 0
Remaining unpaid ... £ 17. 10. 0

Aug 18 / 80

Henry Robinson's 1879 Memorandum of Sale

The first Post Office & General Shop built 1887 by Henry Robinson

The old Post Office today

We see, however, that a few years later, in 1898, a young Flora Timms (later Thompson) arrived in Grayshott, and took a job in the Post Office, being responsible for the telegraph system as well as serving customers.

As a result of this growing interest and favour in the area, the population accordingly grew over the years. In the early 1870s Grayshott could not boast of more than a hundred souls, but by 1901 this had grown more than six-fold to six hundred and sixty-six, with a total of one hundred and forty-three habitable houses. In 1891, with the growth of the local community, it had been felt necessary to build a church, albeit of a temporary nature at the time, constructed mostly of corrugated iron and wood. This was used as the only place of worship that was available in Grayshott for several years, until it was superseded in 1899, when the new church of St. Luke's was completed, as we know it today.

The development and growth of the village was also helped in no small part by the lively and constructive interest that was taken by various influential persons and families at the time, including the I'Ansons, the Whitakers, and the Lyndons amongst others.

The I'Ansons

Edward I'Anson

Mr Edward I'Anson, born on the 25th July 1812, was a renowned Architect, who had the unique

distinction of becoming both President of the Royal Institute of British Architects and also the Surveyor's Institution. These days he is known largely for his involvement in the construction of the Royal Exchange (1842-44), St. Bartholomew's Hospital (1878-79), the school of the Merchant Taylors Company at Charterhouse, the British & Foreign Bible Society, and the Corn Exchange in London (1881).

Edward I'Anson 1812–1888

He married Catherine Blakeway in June 1842 and the couple had five daughters and two sons. Their eldest daughter, Marie-Henrietta, married a Swiss banker from Neuchatel named David de Pury, who, at the time, owned Grayshott House on the corner to Waggoners Wells. Another daughter, Berthe, went on to marry Alexander Ingham Whitaker, and a further daughter, Catherine, born in 1847, remained unmarried throughout her life but was nevertheless to become a major contributor to the life of the village, as we shall see shortly.

In 1861, Edward bought what was then known as the Grayshott Park Estate, being a seventy-five acre portion of the lots arising out of the earlier Enclosure legislation, which was to be found on the south side of Headley Road, between Ruffit Lane and Grayshott House. The price he paid was One Hundred and Thirty-Seven Pounds.

It was said at the time that, in order to view the property, he rode on horseback all the way from Clapham Common to Grayshott, and was pleased with what he saw.

Stopping at the Royal Huts Hotel on the Portsmouth Road in Hindhead for rest and refreshment he was, however, warned that the whole area was wild and lawless, and that he would never succeed in building there. The author Thomas Wright, in "Hindhead, or the English Switzerland" in 1898, was of the opinion "that he would not succeed in completing it or in living there, the few cottagers and squatters of the hamlet bearing the character of being lawless folk who would never allow a stranger to settle among them".

The predecessors of the squatters were known as:

> "Runagates, i.e. persons who had fled from justice and the law, and in the dense woodland they skulk like the badger or the fox".

The Hindhead Gang, as previously mentioned, was a notorious group of ne'er-do-wells, based in Hindhead and Grayshott at the time, which roamed the countryside, robbing and terrorising travellers and stealing sheep from the isolated farms. These sheep stealers lived mainly in the two valleys, Stoney Bottom and Whitmoor Vale and, if and when they were ever caught and brought to justice, they would often be subject to transportation, usually to Australia, for life.

In Stoney Bottom, it was known that the sheep stealers had large hogsheads or vats for storing the mutton. These were cunningly divided into two separate compartments, one of which contained the mutton, and the other (much smaller one) contained mead which was offered as refreshment to allay the suspicions of any officers of the law who might pass by, on the lookout for stolen carcasses.

Squatters were also prevalent in the area, and were a thorn in the side of the authorities. The common practise of squatters was to erect huts in the middle of the night, quickly thatch them, and then place women and children inside. This outwitted the bailiffs sent by the Lord of the Manor, who had no power to remove the roof of any building in which children were to be found. To achieve this, it was quite common for children to be "borrowed" from neighbours for this purpose.

Earlier, in 1822, William Cobbett, a native of Farnham and a well-known writer and social reformer, who travelled on horseback widely in the area and beyond, was depressed enough to say that the area "is certainly the most villainous spot that God ever created".

However, as Mr Wright acknowledged, Edward I'Anson was not put off. He bought the land, and built a grand house, known as Heather Lodge, in 1862 and lived there for many years, in peace and harmony with his supposedly suspicious and dodgy neighbours.

Indeed, in 1867, Alfred Tennyson, the famed poet, took a lease of nearby Grayshott Farm, later to become Grayshott Hall. He wrote at the time to a friend saying that he had been warned about the dangerous local inhabitants, and that he was putting himself in danger. In spite of this, his time in Grayshott was a successful one, and he left with good heart, having compiled many memorable poems during his stay.

Whilst Edward I'Anson was living at Heather Lodge the house was, interestingly, also to be used as the distribution centre for the local mail, brought there by horse from Petersfield, prior to the establishment of a Post Office in the village.

It was he who, shortly after, gave a piece of land to the Parish, which enabled the new National School to be built in 1871, where it stands today in School Road. He also took on the role of School Correspondent (Inspector) and Treasurer of the school for many years, taking a very keen interest in the welfare and the running of the village school.

He died unexpectedly on 30th January 1888, and was buried in the cemetery at All Saints Church in Headley.

After his death, Heather Lodge was sold to a Mr & Mrs Charles Vertue, both devoted Roman Catholics, who renamed the house "Grayshott Court". As we shall see later, "The Court", as it was known, was to become a centre for devout local Catholics in the local community, on the road out of the village towards Headley.

In 1912, Mrs Vertue, by that time a widow, gave the house to the Order of Our Lady of the Cenacle, and it became The Convent of the Cenacle, close to where the current church of St. Joseph's is situated today.

The Convent provided sterling service during the Great War of 1914–1918, when it opened its doors as a private hospital for sick and wounded soldiers. As a sub hospital to the Cambridge Military Hospital in Aldershot, it was staffed by local doctors and nurses, and provided a fully equipped hospital facility for the needs of many hundreds of military personnel.

The Cenacle was finally sold for redevelopment in 1999 and demolished. The site is now occupied entirely by private housing that is located off Headley Road before the Waggoners Wells turning.

Edward Blakeway I'Anson.

Mr Edward Blakeway I'Anson, the son of Edward, was born on 28th June 1843. As with all his siblings, he took his mother's maiden name of Blakeway as part of his own name. Over the years he became a successful architect like his father, eventually taking over his father's business at 7a, Laurence Pountney in the City of London.

Edward I'Anson 1843–1912

Also, like his father, he became a prominent figure in the early development of Grayshott village. He was, for example, a member of the local committee that was set up in order to raise funds for the construction of St. Luke's Church in the 1890s. He gave his services free as Honorary Architect of the church, and was also responsible for the addition of the spire to the church, which was completed later in 1910. Edward also inaugurated the I'Anson Cup Competition in cricket, which is still competed for to this day in Grayshott and surrounding villages. He never married, and he was buried in St. Luke's churchyard on the 15th December 1912.

Catherine Blakeway I'Anson.

Catherine I'Anson was one of the daughters of Edward I'Anson, who, as we have said, was responsible for the foundation of the Grayshott National School in 1871. She, like her family, was a major contributor to village life, and very active in the formation of a number of its institutions. She was devoted to the welfare of the village, and particularly to the children. Catherine very largely financed the running of the school herself in its early years, and was a regular visitor, acting as school's Attendance Officer. She often came to the school for days on end, not only to inspect the registers but also to involve herself in the children's schoolwork, to hear lessons, and indeed often to give lessons as well.

A formidable figure, she was both feared and respected in equal measure by the children. She was instantly recognisable in the village, as she always walked around dressed in a long black coat and black velvet bonnet, regardless of the weather, carrying an umbrella, but always with a kindly and friendly smile on her face.

She could be rather frightening to the younger children, either in School or in Church. She had a disconcerting habit of poking her umbrella into the ribs of any child she thought to be lazy or naughty; but behind the frightening exterior there was a woman with a warm and considerate heart, who took the welfare of her charges very seriously.

She gave the land on which St. Luke's Church is built and, adjoining this, also gave the land where the original laundry was built (now The Pottery). It was her wish and intention that the laundry could provide employment for girls leaving the school next door.

Catherine I'Anson 1847–1916

She died on Friday, 2nd June 1916. Her funeral and burial took place at St. Luke's on the 6th June, coincidentally on the same day when the village sadly learned of the death of Lord Kitchener. The church was filled to capacity with mourners, including almost all of the children of the school which she had founded.

The Grayshott Parish Magazine at the time stated: "The site of the Church and Vicarage, the school buildings and their maintenance are the expressions and symbols of a heartfelt dedication to the life of Grayshott which only the affection of those who have known her will properly understand".

It has been said that her ghost today haunts the store room in the school building. Several persons claim to have seen it, and that the face of the ghost strongly resembles that of Catherine. Maybe she is still keeping her eye on the children?

The Whitakers

In 1884, the Whitakers came to Grayshott, when Mr Joseph Whitaker Senior bought Grayshott Farm, as it was then known. The sales catalogue produced by a noted London estate agent described it as a "picturesque modern residence or small mansion…well and substantially erected of Bargate stone (quarried on the estate) with red brick dressings and weather tiles and strong red tiled roofs". There was "a good carriage drive, a large level lawn and walled kitchen garden, and a large ornamental entrance lodge".

Joseph Whitaker himself was a successful businessman and wine importer, having large estates both in Yorkshire and Palermo, Italy, as we have seen, and he took it upon himself in the late 1880s to buy estates for each of his three sons.

His eldest son, Alexander Ingham Whitaker, was to become the owner of what became Grayshott Hall in 1886, and soon after assuming ownership he put in hand an ambitious programme of extension and reconstruction work, including the construction of a small tower there.

The 1891 census records show that Mr Whitaker lived at the Hall together with a housekeeper, cook, four housemaids, a butler, footman and a houseboy.

In 1895, he married Berthe DePury, the eldest daughter of Mr David DePury, who originated from Switzerland and lived in nearby Grayshott House, in Headley Road. Berthe was in fact the granddaughter of Edward I'Anson and niece of Miss Catherine I'Anson.

Alexander Ingham Whitaker
1857–1933

Whilst Alexander and Berthe lived in Grayshott, they took a very active part in the growth and development of the village. They were regarded as most public-spirited, and took major roles in the running of the village school, the building of St. Luke's Church, and the village hall, of which Mr Whitaker became a Trustee. He was a Parish councillor for Headley from 1894 to 1908, a member of Grayshott Parish Council from 1902, becoming Chairman in 1908 until he left the village in 1927. He also served as a Justice of the Peace and became High Sheriff of the Country of Southampton in March 1919. Amongst other things, he gave three acres of land to the village between 1902 and 1920, originally for the use of the land as allotments but later used as playing fields, and in 1919 a ten-acre field which is the current playing field in Headley Road.

During the Whitaker's time, Grayshott Hall hosted numerous events connected with the village. Within the grounds of the Hall there was a cricket ground which was used by the active village cricket club, team members including such names as Arthur Conan Doyle, John McMillan, later to become Bishop of Guildford, Mr Whitaker himself, Bert Chapman and other local residents.

As well as cricket matches, there were a number of annual events held at the Hall and in the grounds. These included the annual Band of Mercy show, Christmas parties for the school children, annual sports days and a tea party attended by nearly a thousand guests to celebrate the coronation of Edward VII. Each year the children of the village were presented with a mug, on which was inscribed "Grayshott Hall" and the year in question.

Having eventually sold Grayshott Hall in 1927, the couple moved to Belgium, and he died in 1933. He is buried in St. Luke's churchyard. Berthe, for her part, returned to live in Redcroft, in Grayshott where she lived until her own death in May 1956.

As for Grayshott Hall, it passed through a number of ownerships from the 1920s onwards, remaining in private hands until 1960. It was then converted into a Health Club, which opened in 1965. Further development of the building has taken place over the years, and it is now the Grayshott Spa, as we know it to be.

Grayshott Hall from an etching

The Lyndons

Doctor Arnold Lyndon and his wife Charlotte moved to Grayshott in the mid 1890s, when they lived at Windwhistle House, a comfortable house with a long drive off Crossways Road. They were both major benefactors to the village and took an active interest in its welfare.

Doctor Arnold Lyndon

During the First World War, the Lyndons helped to run the military hospital at the Convent of the Cenacle, from 1914 through to 1918, he being the Medical Superintendent and she the Lady Superintendent. They were instrumental in ensuring the smooth running of the hospital, and many wounded soldiers were to benefit hugely from the attention and care that the Lyndon's work was able to provide. In recognition of his work, Arnold Lyndon received an OBE in May 1920.

Mrs Lyndon was one of the originators of the scheme which led to the opening of the Fox and Pelican under the Temperance Peoples Refreshment House Association, of which she became the Chairwoman. She was also unpaid Clerk to Grayshott Parish council from 1902 until 1928, and Chairwoman until her death in 1936. She was also a Justice of the Peace, representing Grayshott for many years on the Alton Board of Guardians and Alton District Council. It was said of her at the time that "she always seemed to be bicycling against the wind and giving out a preoccupied smile. But she was a great hand, it is said, at parochial matters, at meditation on the bicycle between meetings and enquiries, and at speaking up for the accused at petty sessions". She was noted to be a shy person, but she did many acts of generosity by stealth.

Doctor Charlotte Lyndon

Charlotte Lyndon died in October 1936, while on holiday in Shrewsbury. One of the wreaths at her funeral read: "She lit a candle in many a dark room". Doctor Lyndon passed away in November 1946.

Charitable Trusts were set up by the Lyndons on their deaths, to provide for charitable assistance where needed in the village, and these charities still exist today, to the continued benefit of various aspects of village life.

Miss (Mary Julia) James

Miss James, born in 1831, was another major benefactor of the village. When she was in her mid-fifties, she moved to Hindhead, and built Westdown, a substantial house to the north east of Grayshott.

Miss Marian James

A benefactor of many local causes, she gave land at both Nutcombe and Bramshott to the then fledgling National Trust in 1908, and was instrumental in securing the acquisition of Ludshott Common by the Trust, by giving a generous personal donation.

She was on the original committee which organised the appeal for funds to build St. Luke's and she also gave a sizeable donation herself to the fund. She was well known in the village for organising, amongst other things, the annual Chamber Music concerts in the Village Hall.

Miss James, together with a Mr & Mrs Bulley, was also responsible for the building of the hostel (now known as Shannon Court) at Bramshott Chase, to provide periods of rest and relaxation for people in the professions, including actors, musicians and teachers. She was also generous in making a gift of some cottages, known as Whitmore Vale Cottages, to the Parish.

She died on the 10th November, 1910. Her memory today is secured with the nearby Miss James Bridge, which gives safe access to pedestrians, cyclists and horse riders along a newly designated bridleway which straddles the A3 cutting south of the Hindhead Tunnel.

CHAPTER THREE

GRAYSHOTT – Of Services and Socials.

THE FOX AND PELICAN

The Fox & Pelican circa 1901

It may seem strange that the village pub in Grayshott came before the village Church, albeit only just. The pub was formally opened for business on 23rd August 1899, and St. Luke's was first used for services some three months later, on Sunday the 17th October 1899. Indeed, St. Joseph's Church was even longer in coming, not being consecrated until a decade later, in 1911.

The pressure had in fact come the previous year, in 1898, when some of the leading Grayshott residents became aware that a new public house was proposed to be built by a Mr Gerald Hall and his brother, both brewers, of Alton, on land where the village green now stands (which was then just a small scruffy field). The Hall brothers were well-known in the area, and with a solid reputation in the trade, could already claim seventy-two public houses to their name. These were mostly in Hampshire, the nearest to Grayshott being the Holly Bush at Headley, still there today.

This "threat", as it were, to the village led to the formation of the Grayshott & District Refreshment Association, organised and run by a village trust. The Association put forward a proposal, which was to establish a privately-run refreshment house, selling both alcoholic and non-alcoholic beverages, run along largely temperance lines. An application for a Justices Licence was made to the local Licensing Justices on this basis, and it was successful. On the other hand, however, the application made at the same time by the Hall brothers for their own proposed public house was in fact turned down.

The land where the pub now stands was acquired and local builders Chapman & Puttick quoted a sum of £1,465 for the building work, excluding the fitting-out costs. The money was raised by the issue of shares, the sixty-eight total shareholders including such well-known local names as George Bernard Shaw, the playwright, Sir Frederick Pollock, the eminent jurist, Mrs Charlotte Lyndon and others. It was not long before construction was put in hand.

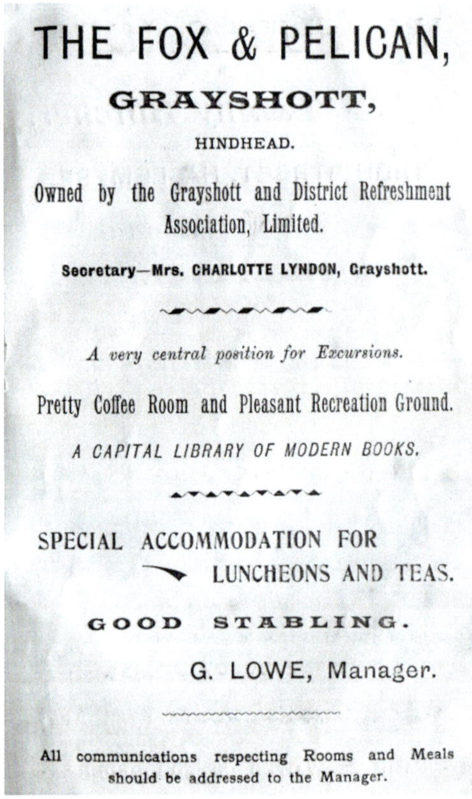

THE FOX & PELICAN,

GRAYSHOTT,

HINDHEAD.

Owned by the Grayshott and District Refreshment Association, Limited.

Secretary—Mrs. CHARLOTTE LYNDON, Grayshott.

A very central position for Excursions.

Pretty Coffee Room and Pleasant Recreation Ground.

A CAPITAL LIBRARY OF MODERN BOOKS.

SPECIAL ACCOMMODATION FOR LUNCHEONS AND TEAS.

GOOD STABLING.

G. LOWE, Manager.

All communications respecting Rooms and Meals should be addressed to the Manager.

A local welcome, in early years

Tennis in the Fox & Pelican garden in the 1920s

The intention of the venture was that, despite it being a licenced building, it was to sell as little alcohol as possible, with the strong emphasis being on alcoholic-free drinks. Following temperance principles, the main profit was to be earned from non-alcoholic drinks and accommodation, with the sales of ales giving the landlord no commission at all, which meant that he had no incentive to promote the sale of beers and spirits on the premises. Also, the landlord had to keep the alcohol out of sight, under the counter, and only sell it when specifically requested by his customers.

"What's in a name – why Fox and Pelican?"

The chairman of the Grayshott and District Refreshment Association was Sir Frederick Pollock who in 1898 was a member of Corpus Christi College. The founder of the college originally was Bishop Fox of Winchester, and the college coat of arms included a pelican. The new pub was in the Winchester diocese, so it seemed appropriate. Simple really.

The new public house was formally opened on 23rd August 1899, by Mrs Randall Davidson, wife of the Bishop of Winchester, in the presence of a large and distinguished company. The opening also attracted a lot of national interest in the country, with reviews and comments appearing in the Daily Telegraph, the London Morning Leader, The Herald and others.

An article appearing in a national newspaper at the time said that: "At the top of a purple Surrey hill, four miles up from the nearest railway station, stands the Fox & Pelican, the newest, and perhaps the prettiest little inn in the world. Yesterday it opened its bar and its coffee-room, its bedrooms and its library, to the thirsty traveller, and thereupon did a trade which kept Mr Wallace (late Steward on "HMS Sanspareil") and his wife busier than they have been for many a day".

It was noted that the rooms had been furnished under the supervision of a Mrs McMillan, who was the widow of the well-known publisher, and that Mr George Bernard Shaw had also contributed by donating a small library of books for the pub's customers use.

A booklet later produced proudly stated that: "The Fox & Pelican enjoys the distinction of being one of the very few hotels the granting of whose licence has received the wholehearted support of a bishop!"

However, despite its opening and general founding principles attracting fulsome praise from many quarters, the pub found it difficult to establish and maintain itself along the lines required by its original shareholders, although it was by no means a failure. It kept going for many years along the largely temperance lines that had been originally proposed, but it did attract a degree of local criticism over its reforming character.

There were, for example, arguments over its Sunday closing time. On one occasion, the manager had decided that this was 8pm, whereas the normal closing time for pubs on a Sunday was 10pm. This had the result that, one evening, it attracted a sit-in by frustrated local residents who refused to leave after 8pm, although they were not served with any beer.

Another difficulty was the frequent change of managers. The first, Mr Wallace, only stayed a short while, and thereafter there were six managers between 1899 & 1904, one of whom successfully sued the owners for the return of his deposit. Another was fined 10 shillings (50p) for dishonestly watering down the whisky. It was obviously difficult to maintain the pub's popularity when it was following a business model which, to a certain extent, ran contrary to the ethos of a normal drinking establishment.

"The original signboard"

The original signboard of the pub was designed and painted in 1899 by Walter Crane, who was a student of the artist John Ruskin. Some years later, in 1913, it was taken down and replaced. It was then hung in the Village Hall by the Parish Council, where it was put on display.

When the First World War broke out in 1914, the hall was handed over to the military in order to provide billeting for the soldiers. It is believed that, at that point, the sign was taken down and returned to the pub for storage purposes. During a general clear out and refurbishment in the 1960s, it passed into private ownership, and disappeared from view for many years.

It was only in recent times that it came up for auction at the showrooms of the Essex auctioneers Messrs Sworders, who confirmed that they had been consigned what then turned out to be the original pub sign from a vendor in Wales. It was happily bought by the Grayshott Pottery Community Fund for £4,300, to be returned and displayed. The signboard came back to the village, and today it can be seen, proudly hung in the main shop premises of the Pottery.

The Fox & Pelican continued under its then present ownership until 1913, when it was sold to the national People's House Refreshment Association, who held it until the late 1950s. when it was taken over by Gales Brewery.

It is now owned and run successfully by the Fullers Brewery, one of its chain of pubs. It serves three regular beers, and has a full restaurant licence as well as having an attractive pub garden, with play area and also considerable parking.

The Fox & Pelican continues today to be a focus of village life, located centrally in the village, and attracting families and individuals with its warm and genial atmosphere.

"Fox & Pelican – The Titanic Connection"

Charlotte Holme was the wife of James Ashbrooke Holme, the pub manager from 1914. She had been one of the few survivors of the tragic sinking of the Titanic in April 1912, along with her daughter Marjorie Lottie. Her then husband Harvey Collyer drowned when the ship went down, leaving them both to be rescued by the SS Carpathia and taken to New York. His body was never recovered.

Friends of Charlotte and Harvey had emigrated to America some years earlier, and had made a success of a fruit farm in Payette, Idaho. They wrote enthusiastically of the warm weather and, as Charlotte was a tuberculosis sufferer at the time, they decided to join their friends in the same valley and buy a farm.

RMS Titanic 1912

The family sold up in England, with Harvey Collyer taking the drastic decision of putting their entire savings, in bank notes, in the inside breast pocket of his jacket for the journey. The remainder of their personal possessions were kept in the Titanic's hold, representing everything the Collyers owned in the world.

Charlotte was in bed in their cabin at the time of impact with the iceberg, feeling nauseous due to some over-rich food they had eaten in the restaurant. Her husband went to investigate and reported back that "there is no danger – an officer just told me". This was not to be, as we now sadly know, and Charlotte and Marjorie were, shortly after, rescued in Titanic's lifeboat number 14, but her husband was never to be seen again, presumed drowned.

She arrived with Marjorie in America, completely destitute, with no clothes other than what they were wearing at the time, and no money. She was forced to survive purely on charity, and also on writing occasional articles for newspapers and magazines about her ordeal. It is interesting to note that one of the articles written by her was used by the writer Walter Lord as source material for his successful book "A Night To Remember", later turned into an Oscar winning film in 1958 and starring Kenneth More.

Charlotte and Marjorie were sadly not able to settle in the United States, but decided to return to Leatherhead in England and to her dead husband's family. The hymn "Nearer My God To Thee", famously sung by crew and passengers as the ship went down, was her favourite when sung in

Leatherhead Parish Church, where Harvey had been the church sexton and verger before they decided to emigrate.

Later on, in 1914, she met and then married James Holme, the landlord of the Fox & Pelican, and settled down in Grayshott, as a publican's wife.

By all accounts her time in Grayshott was a happy one, although she never really recovered from her ordeal. She sadly died of tuberculosis on 28th November 1916, at the early age of only thirty-five. It can only be imagined how her weakened system must have suffered from enduring more than seven freezing hours in an open lifeboat in the middle of the icy Atlantic.

Her second husband, James, himself died less than three years later, on March 22nd 1919, leaving little Marjorie to be brought up by her uncle Walter Collyer, a gamekeeper.

Charlotte was buried in the churchyard of St. Mary's, in Bishopstoke, near Eastleigh, where her gravestone is still prominent today. It is understood that there are still descendants of the family living in the Leatherhead area to this day.

Charlotte Holme, then Collyer & Marjorie destitute in America. Note the 'White Star Line' blanket

GRAYSHOTT SCHOOL

The school at Grayshott was the first public institution to appear in the village – before any of the Churches, the Village Hall, even the Fox and Pelican pub.

Prior to the Education Act of 1870 the provision of education for young people was an uncoordinated and unregulated arrangement. The National Society (of Anglican disposition) had been founded in 1811 with the intention of setting up National Schools wherever possible. This movement towards universal education grew as time passed and by the mid 1850s there were believed to be in the order of seventeen thousand schools in England and Wales, all providing a basic education in reading and writing for young children.

This albeit somewhat haphazard arrangement was ultimately formalised with the passing of the Education Act of 1870 through Parliament, which, for the first time, laid down the framework for a national system of basic education, allowing for an elementary education to be made available for all children between the ages of five and ten years.

Grayshott School today

Miss Catherine I'Anson, to whom we have referred earlier, first established a Sunday School for local children, held in a room of the laundry that was attached to her house "Heather Lodge". However, by 1871 the population of Grayshott was growing, and the number of young families increasing in the area made it more difficult for local children, who up to now had to travel to Headley to receive any form of education. As a result, her father Edward I'Anson came forward and generously provided land on which to build a one-roomed school with lobby, on the site where the present school now stands.

The school, consisting of just one room and a lobby, was formally opened (as "Grayshott National School") on 4th September 1871, in the presence of some forty dignitaries and local residents. On that first day there was a total of just seven pupils in attendance, although a further eight were added by the end of the month. The numbers rapidly increased, to twenty-six by the end of 1871, thirty-nine in 1872, and sixty-seven in 1873. By the year 1908 there were one hundred and eighty-three on the register, and by January 1910 this had risen by almost a third again, to two hundred and thirty-five.

Grayshott School pupils 8–9 years

As the popularity of the school increased, so the buildings were improved and extended over the years. The first enlargement of the school was in 1878/9, and soon afterwards, a new schoolroom was built. Further extension work was undertaken in 1900 and thereafter at various stages, for the school to be viewed largely as it appears today.

Initially, a charge was levied at the rate of a penny a week for the first child of the family and a halfpenny per week for any additional family members, the money said to be "belonging to the Mistress and forming part of her salary". Where families were experiencing real poverty, however, those fees were often wholly or partly remitted. In May 1875 the fees were raised to three pennies a week for all children, but two pennies of this was to be returned at the end of the school year to the parents of children who had made more than two hundred and fifty attendances in that time. School fees were not completely abolished by law until 1892.

The first teacher was Mrs Esther Clark, a widow with two young children, who had recently moved to Grayshott from Brighton. She stayed until 1885 when she left upon her marriage to a fellow teacher, Mr F E Child, who had joined the school in 1883.

She was regarded as a firm but fair teacher, who could be somewhat magisterial in her attitude towards both her pupils and their parents alike. She was not above dispensing corporal punishment when it was deemed necessary, and she was not hesitant in addressing her feelings to a child's parents when she felt that the pupil in question was not achieving his or her potential.

She also took a keen interest in the welfare of the children. An entry in the School Log of 28th May 1881 reads: "The children came to school in a dirty untidy state with unwashed hands and faces and ragged frocks, jackets and pinafores. They were told to come cleaner tomorrow and to ask for pieces with which to patch their clothes as patches were better than holes". The reprimand obviously worked as the entry for the following day stated that the children were of much better appearance.

One problem in particular that concerned the school was the question of absenteeism. Attendance at school was not made compulsory until 1876, and absences were frequent, especially in the summer months when many children were expected to help their parents at harvest time in the fields. This was anticipated by the school, and the summer holidays were arranged, as far as possible, to minimise this disruption to the system.

The school Log Books, for instance, make frequent references to "herting", i.e. picking whortle-berries. It was clear that children regularly worked locally at harvest time, and that sometimes whole families moved to a more agricultural area for the harvest season, no doubt as a way of supplementing the family's income for the winter.

Esther Clark's general popularity, however, was not in doubt, and she enjoyed a good working relationship with both parents and also the Inspectors of the school. And behind her all the time, in the manner of an overseeing godmother to the school, was the ever-present Catherine I'Anson.

The school buildings themselves remained in the ownership of the I'Anson family until 1914, and throughout, Catherine I'Anson took a close and personal interest in the running of the school, more so in her position as an Inspector. She devoted a vast amount of her time on behalf of the school, taking a major role in all aspects of the progress of the children and the development of the school in general.

For many years she often visited the school on a daily basis, even taking classes and testing the children. She also carried out annual inspections of each class and wrote a summary report in the School Log following the official school Annual Inspection.

She donated many items to the school, for the benefit of the children, including exercise books, pencils, books, and materials for knitting and needlework, all paid for personally herself. In January 1887, it was noted that she had paid all the school pennies for the week, as a New Year gift for the children. In 1900 it was also noted that she sent a bottle of port to the school, for those children who were suffering from an outbreak of measles at the time. Presumably it did little to remove the spots, but possibly made life a little more bearable.

As the school grew over the years, it became more and more a social centre of the village. The Parish Magazine makes frequent references to concerts taking place there, being well attended by parents and friends. The buildings were also used for meetings of the Church Lads Brigade, the Choral Society, the Orchestral Society and the Band of Mercy.

In October 1900, two days after the newly built St. Luke's church was consecrated, the children and their parents attended a party in the new schoolroom, as Miss I'Anson's guests. Included in the programme, after tea, was a magician who, it was said, "greatly amused the children with such tricks as producing a nosegay of flowers from William Madgwick's head, playing cards from Mr Seeley's waistcoat, taking cigarettes from pockets of a number of innocent looking boys, and pennies from everywhere".

The year 1902 saw the coronation of King Edward VII. There were great celebrations throughout Grayshott. The school and pupils were involved in a huge tea party for nearly a thousand guests that took place in one of the outbuildings of Grayshott Hall, under the supervision of Mr & Mrs Whitaker and Miss I'Anson. A full Sports Day was arranged on the day, and the Grayshott Brass Band played lustily in attendance.

By the end of the reign of Queen Victoria, and the dawn of the new century, the school was firmly established as both a social and educational centre of the village. It contributed much to the development and improvement of the growing population of the village, and rapidly became one of the most important features of Grayshott life.

That it succeeded so well is by no small part attributable to the impetus provided by such strong local personalities as Catherine I'Anson, both in financial as well as practical terms. The legacy of this impetus is still with us today.

ST. LUKE'S CHURCH

The church which is located at the fiveways crossroads of the village was originally going to be called after St. John the Baptist, being the preacher in the wilderness, a reference to the lawless reputation previously enjoyed by the district. The fact that the name was changed to that of St. Luke, who was the patron saint of medicine and physicians, is said to have been influenced by Dr Arnold Lyndon, who took a very active interest in local affairs at the time. This is, however, purely speculation.

Originally, the district of what we know as Grayshott was part of the Parish of Headley, and early residents had to travel four miles or so in order to worship at Headley church. But as Grayshott grew as a community, it became more and more apparent that a local place of worship was required.

As a result of this, in 1873, regular services for parishioners were started in a room at the newly opened Grayshott School, services being taken by the Rector of Headley, the Reverend W.H. Laverty, and later by Canon William W. Capes. This continued for a while, but it soon became apparent that there was a need for more permanent facilities.

Building St Luke's Church

St Luke's Church today

A temporary structure, an "Iron Room", which consisted of a steel framework bolted together with corrugating iron sheeting, was initially erected in Stoney Bottom, funding being provided by Canon Capes and local resident Miss James. This was used for services and meetings up until 1891. As this structure quickly outgrew its usefulness, Mr Alexander Whitaker generously gave funds to build a similar structure on land which is now part of St. Luke's churchyard, at a position between the present vestry and the maintenance shed. This seemed to be satisfactory for a while, as the new venue was slightly more local to the centre of the village and more easily accessible for those wishing to worship. However, with the continuing growth of the population of the village, it became apparent to parishioners that a more permanent structure would be welcomed.

In early 1898, a formal meeting was convened, presided over by Canon Capes, with other well-known local residents in attendance including Alexander Ingham Whitaker and Edward I'Anson as well as Catherine I'Anson, Miss James, Professor Williamson of High Pitfold and the Reverend J.M. Jeakes. At the meeting an endowment fund was launched, to raise money for the construction of the new church, with an initial target of £6,000.

As well as having to raise the required funds, according to the Reverend Jeakes there followed "long and troublesome negotiations involved in the formation of an ecclesiastical district out of three parishes and two counties". However, these problems were eventually overcome and Grayshott duly became an ecclesiastical parish in its own right.

The church was designed in the "Old English" style and of Bargate stone on the exterior and Headley stone on the interior. It allowed for seating for three hundred and fifty people, and was built one hundred and two feet in length, and forty two feet in width, including the aisles, in the nave. The work was undertaken by local builders Chapman, Lowry & Puttick, who employed a small army of workmen in order to complete the construction on time.

The foundation stone of the new church was laid by Miss I'Anson on 3rd September 1898 with a silver trowel given to her by Mr Whitaker. Sadly, the trowel was stolen from the church in a robbery in recent years.

The first service held in the new church was Holy Communion at 8am on Sunday 17th October 1899, followed by a well-attended 11am service, when Canon Capes gave the Sermon.

Following this, the church was formally consecrated at a service on the eve of the Festival of St. Luke, on Tuesday the 17th October 1900 held by the Bishop of Winchester, Bishop Randall Davidson. The church was packed for the occasion, when the formal consecration was signed, and the deeds of conveyance were handed to the Bishop by Dr. Lyndon. After the service, at the invitation of Mr & Mrs Jeakes, the majority of the five hundred who had attended the service moved to the nearby vicarage for a celebratory tea and dance.

The first wedding to take place in the church was that of James Muir of Chatham, a surgeon serving in the Royal Navy, to Miss Eleanor Pearson, of Grayshott, on 3rd December 1901, who were married by a visiting vicar. The first marriage officiated by Reverend Jeakes was on 25th December, Christmas Day itself, that same year, when Mr James Winchester was married to Miss Kate Wetton.

The church had originally been constructed without a tower and spire. Mr Edward I'Anson's initial design had in fact included a tower, but this was not completed at the time of construction, for various reasons. In September 1907, however, a further appeal was raised for funds in order to build a new tower, requiring in the order of £1,500, and Mr I'Anson was again commissioned to undertake the design work. By 1910, the appeal fund had received £1,580, so that the work could go ahead.

The decision to complete the project was taken because an anonymous offer had also been made to donate a church clock, to be installed in the tower, provided the project proceeded with all due speed.

Again, Chapman, Lowry & Puttick were employed to undertake the work. The new tower and spire were built, together with a clock and three bells for striking the hours and quarters, in the manner which exists today.

On 1st November 1910, the Bishop of Guildford attended a Service of Dedication of the new construction. Sadly, only two years later Mr I'Anson died, leaving a fitting legacy of his contributions to the life of the village.

ST. JOSEPH'S ROMAN CATHOLIC CHURCH

The Church of St. Joseph, along the Headley Road, was not actually built until a decade or so after St. Luke's. But the area where it stands was, for some time earlier, a centre for religious teachings and learnings. This was largely due to the activities of the Vertue family, and, in particular, Mrs Ada Vertue, a truly remarkable lady.

She arrived in Grayshott in 1887 after her marriage to Charles Erskine Vertue, a Government Inspector of Schools, who was also an Honorary Chamberlain to Pope Pius X. The newly-wed couple set up home at The Court, in Headley Road, which they had acquired from Edward I'Anson. The house was formerly called Heather Lodge, and in later years it became The Convent of our Lady of the Cenacle.

St Joseph's Church, an early photograph

In the early days of their living in Grayshott, the Vertues attended Mass, somewhat unusually, at a nearby neighbour's house. Sir Archibald Keppel Macdonald was the owner of Woolmer Lodge, to be found along Woolmer Lane, between Ludshott Common and Bramshott. He had constructed a small Catholic chapel there, to adjoin the main house, for his own use and benefit.

The Vertues visited Sir Archibald frequently but the journey was not easy, as it was a fairly difficult horse-drawn drive along a rough road over the Common. In November 1890, the Bishop of Portsmouth came to the village to give Confirmation to Charles Vertue, and to say Mass at Sir Archibald's little chapel.

Whilst he was there he suggested to the Vertues that, in future, Mass could be held once a week at their house, the Court, rather than having to travel to Woolmer Lodge. This was eagerly agreed upon, but, very sadly, just two weeks later there was a very serious fire at The Court, and the building was almost totally destroyed.

Despite the tragedy, the Vertues decided to rebuild the house, and the Bishop suggested that a small chapel could be incorporated into the rebuild, in order for a daily Mass to be held. This was duly done, and the new building of The Court was completed on June 26th 1895, being the Feast of St. John and St. Paul. After the chapel was opened, the number of local people attending services gradually grew over the years, until about thirty or so could be counted as regular worshippers.

Grayshott at the time was growing as a village community and, with nearby houses and boarding houses being built to cater for increased numbers of visitors, together with more and more houses being constructed, the demand for different venues for worship in the area grew. In 1902, for example, a census of the local Catholic population showed that there were ten males, twenty-two females and nineteen children, the latter being those that had not taken their first communion.

After Charles Vertue died in 1904, his wife spent more and more time away from the village. Despite this, she was determined not to give up The Court until there was a proper church to take its place, such was the continuing popularity of the chapel that they had constructed there. So much so that on Easter Sunday 1909, over one hundred people attended Mass in the chapel, where there was not only standing room only, but the congregation also overspilled into adjacent rooms.

It was soon after this service that a Father John, one of the Franciscans who had previously served the congregation, visited Mrs Vertue. Over several discussions it was decided that Grayshott should indeed have its own permanent Catholic church, in place of the chapel which was struggling to serve the needs of the local community.

The Bishop's consent was obtained, and Mrs Vertue duly allocated some land within the grounds of The Court for a church to be built, together with a presbytery and churchyard. Built in the Gothic style, the church was constructed with stone walls and two buttresses on the north side, a tiled roof, parallel lower roofs above both the north and south chapels and a stone bell turret over the chancel, all in the perpendicular 15th century style. The nave was built with four bays and a porch on the north side.

The new church, named after St. Joseph, was eventually completed, and consecrated by the Right Reverend W. Cotter, the Bishop of Portsmouth, at a service on the Feast of St. Anne, 26th July, 1911. The consecration ceremony was attended by a very large crowd of worshippers, followed by High Mass and, afterwards, the many visitors were entertained by Mrs Vertue to tea, and introduced personally to the Bishop.

Following the consecration of St. Joseph's, Mrs Vertue continued with her husband's work of inviting sick priests to stay and rest at The Court. This led her to think of converting The Court into a permanent House of Retreat, which could be used as a place of rest, recovery and meditation. The major stumbling block to this idea was that the available accommodation made the idea impracticable. After further considering the problem, and keen to make a lasting contribution to the Church, she approached the Reverend Mother D'Angliano of Our Lady of the Cenacle with the idea of making an absolute gift of The Court to the Order.

This offer was gladly accepted, The Court duly changed hands on 26th April 1913, and thereafter became known as the Convent of our Lady of the Cenacle.

It was thereafter occupied by the Order's nuns, who remained in residence for over eighty years, until shortly before it was demolished in 1999 to be replaced with residential housing. Following the change of ownership, Mrs Vertue, then in her late 50s, moved to St. Anne's in Headley Road.

Mrs Vertue died on 28th November 1934 aged seventy-nine and is buried in St. Joseph's churchyard. As a permanent Memorial to this redoubtable lady, a Memorial Fund was established and, out of this, a stained-glass window was installed above the High Altar of the church and dedicated to her memory.

GRAYSHOTT METHODIST CHURCH

To many people in Grayshott, the village has only ever enjoyed the benefit of two churches, namely St. Luke's and St. Joseph's, serving the Protestant and Catholic communities respectively. What is less well known is that a third church in fact took root in the village, forming part of village life for over seventy years, and was furthermore located close to the very heart of the shopping centre in Headley Road itself.

The Methodist Church in Headley Road

The Grayshott Methodist Church, also known as the Wesleyan Mission Chapel, was built in 1901 and opened in November of that year. It was built in the first place as a temporary iron structure, being sheathed in corrugated tin sheeting, and was built at a cost of £170 by Messrs Humphreys of Knightsbridge.

Flats on the Methodist Church site today

It operated as a fully-functioning church for over seventy years until it was eventually demolished in the late 1970s. During the period of the First World War, the building was taken over by Grayshott School, for temporary use as a school room, when the school's own building itself was taken over by the military, before the troops left for France and the Western Front.

No trace of the building exists today, and in its place there now stands a building comprising a number of modern flats, known as Oaklea House.

GRAYSHOTT VILLAGE HALL

The Village Hall is believed to be the biggest village hall in Hampshire. Situated just on the county boundary between Hampshire and Surrey, on the Headley Road leading up to the A3, it has provided a comprehensive facility in the village for a diverse range of clubs, societies and groups for over a hundred years.

Its beginnings originated from meetings and social gatherings that took place in the old Iron Room (referred to earlier) located in Stoney Bottom at the end of the 19th century. This was a popular venue, but with the growth of the village it was not long before it became obvious that it was quite inadequate for the purpose.

Grayshott Village Hall in 1902

In June 1900, a note appeared in the Parish Magazine stating: "Many of us have long felt that the present Iron Room which still serves many useful purposes, has for some time been inadequate to meet the growing needs of the village. As there seemed no immediate hope of anything more adequate, little has been done about it. We are now pleased to announce that a most generous offer of £500 has been received towards this object provided that a suitable site can be procured, and the rest of the money raised, so that building may commence fairly soon."

As a result of this a meeting was held on 18th July 1900 to discuss plans for the establishment of a Village Hall and Club for Grayshott and its neighbourhood. It was originally planned to hold the meeting in the Iron Room itself, but, because it was such a hot day, it was adjourned to "a shady glade in the fir woods of Mrs Anderson Wells".

Over thirty people attended the meeting, which was chaired by Mr Marshall Bulley. A working committee was appointed, with Trustees, which included Mr Bulley, Mr John McMillan (who was to become Bishop of Guildford), Mr Alexander Ingham Whitaker, and representatives from Hampshire County Council. An appeal for donations was made and by September a further £143 had been raised in addition to the original £500.

In January 1901, two pieces of land situated on the corner of Boundary Road with Headley Road were acquired from a Mrs Plympton-Smith, who lived at Hurstmere. She agreed to sell the land for the very reasonable sum of £100, in memory of her brother Dr Richard Plympton, who had sadly died in December 1899 at the young age of 45, and who had been a pioneering expert in the development of X-rays.

The site was then conveyed to the Trustees and, by the autumn of 1901 work had commenced on the laying of foundations, even though funding was not yet finally in place. The building work was undertaken by local builders Chapman, Lowry and Puttick, whose tender for the work was £3,430. By May 1902, the work was complete.

A notice was published in the Parish Magazine that there was to be an official opening ceremony in the evening of Thursday 23rd May 1902 and, following the official opening of the new Village Hall, a programme of entertainment followed, provided by the Grayshott Dramatic Society, the String Band and the Choral Society.

The Hall, originally called the "Grayshott and Hindhead Institute and Village Hall", very quickly gained in popularity, developing as an important social hub to the village, and providing facilities for a variety of interests and societies to thrive and grow. Within a short time it was being used for, amongst other things, Technical classes, Gymnasium classes, musical drill, Choral Society, Orchestral Society, and numerous lectures. It became the centre for many organisations in the village, as well as the offices of the newly formed Parish Council.

In November 1902 the Hall was full to overflowing when a party from Miss Aggie Weston's "Sailor's Rest" in Portsmouth presented an evening of "The Bluejackets in the Fo'cle", with total ticket sales amounting to a healthy £17.

Lectures were frequently given on a wide range of subjects, and were given by both local people as well as invited speakers from elsewhere. As an example, a talk was given to a packed-out audience in February 1914 by Mr Apsley Cherry-Garrard, who had been a member of Captain Robert Falcon Scott's team on the ill-fated Terra Nova Expedition of 1910–1912 to the South Pole. Many lectures were illustrated with the use of a borrowed limelight lantern or oil lantern.

In January 1904 it was suggested that an electric lantern be purchased by the Hall for an estimated cost of £30, which would also include a screen for viewing pictures. This innovation was eagerly approved, and the first lecture using the new lantern was given on the 7th October 1904.

As early as the spring of 1906, it was apparent that the high level of use of the Hall warranted an extension being built, to accommodate the growing numbers, and it was decided to build additional rooms on the side of the existing building. Work began in the July on what was to become known as the Small Hall, which allowed for additional uses of the Village Hall, including that of a Library, closed only in recent years.

In April 1907, the Trustees proposed that ownership of the building be passed over to Grayshott Parish Council, as it was by now clear that the Village Hall was truly an asset of the village. It seemed only appropriate that the Hall should become owned by the elected representatives of the village itself, and once a number of conditions had been satisfied, the Conveyance dated 20th August 1907 duly confirmed the transfer of ownership to the Parish Council.

Today, the Village Hall continues to provide an extensive and flexible venue for all manner of interests, together with a large stage, equipped to full theatrical standards, as well as providing rehearsal rooms, offices, changing rooms, and a fully-equipped kitchen. It is truly a valuable and important asset to the village.

GRAYSHOTT FIRE SERVICE

By the early years of the 20th century, Grayshott was growing apace, with an ever-increasing number of houses and shops to serve the burgeoning population. As a result, there was anxiety about the very real possibility of fire damage to life and property, especially in an area which was surrounded by common land, where fires could be frequent in the dry summer months. George Bernard Shaw had already made reference to this in a letter which he wrote to the local paper in March 1899, and it was clear that concern was growing.

As a result, in 1906, it was decided that the Grayshott and Hindhead Fire Brigade should be formed, using a wooden building that was erected on the frontage to Headley Road, close by the Village Hall. The service was initially established with voluntary contributions of £129, which was used to buy nine hydrants, as well as twelve hundred feet of hose and a hose cart. Initially there were twelve volunteer firemen, who received free uniforms, and were paid for attending fires at the rate of one shilling an hour, with out-of-pocket expenses being met for horses, callers and assistants. The first fire tenders were pulled by horses, and the animals did sterling service for eleven years, until they were replaced, in 1917, by a motorised fire tender, which cost the grand sum of £55.

The 'new' Grayshott Fire Service circa 1906

Fire at Tarn Moor 19 February 1907

It was not long before the new service was put to its test. On a stormy night of 19th February 1907 the new brigade, with its rudimentary equipment, had its first emergency call. "Tarn Moor", the home of retired solicitor Mr Frederick Jackson, was on fire and a Mr Mitchell, seizing the bell of his butcher's shop, ran up Headley Road, ringing it for all he was worth, and shouting "Fire, fire". The firemen did their best, but their equipment was clearly not up to the job. Not only were their hoses too short, but also the water pressure proved to be inadequate. In the end, the building was almost totally destroyed, although much of the furniture was saved. A baptism of fire, indeed.

The Service has since then survived and grown, and has been a visible asset to the village now for over one hundred years. Back in 1957, the fire service had marked its 50th anniversary with a large celebration held at the Royal Huts Hotel, where speeches were given and many service awards handed out. The old fire station, located on the site of what had previously been the village bowling green, was closed in the summer of 1964, at which time the modern Fire Station, as we now know it, was erected. Being now part of Hampshire Fire Service, it continues to be manned by local part-time firemen on a voluntary basis, and is renowned locally for its rapid turnout and quick arrival at points of danger.

The Fire Service has indeed come a long way in Grayshott since the early days when messengers on foot rallied the crew, who then had to run on foot to the fire, with their horses pulling the hose cart to the scene.

THE BOWLING GREEN/ TENNIS CLUB

When the Village Hall was first developed, there was a large area of lawn on the side of the site, adjacent to Boundary Road. This was initially set aside for use as tennis courts for the village. The Grayshott Tennis Club was set up in November 1911 and, with enclosed wire netting, tennis was played there until 1925. In that year, the club moved to the four new hard courts that were laid on the present site by the recreation ground, and in the following year the land adjoining Boundary Road was converted to a Bowling Green. This was used by the Bowling Club for many years, until the land was eventually sold and became incorporated as part of the new, modern Fire Station, as mentioned above.

GRAYSHOTT AND THE TELEPHONE

It was during this time that the telephone became established in the village. Grayshott's own telephone exchange was located at the Post Office in Crossways Road, where Miss Flora Thompson had previously worked.

The first published list of Grayshott telephone numbers appeared in the National Telephone Company directory of 1907, and is shown here. In this list there are twenty-one subscribers; numbers 13 and 22 were omitted but these were taken up in 1908.

It is interesting to note that some of these original numbers still exist at the same premises today, although modified and expanded over the years.

576

*** GRAYSHOTT.**

The Exchange will be open from 8.0 a.m. to 8.0 p.m. on Week Days, and from 8.0 a.m. to 10.0 a.m. on Sundays.

The Sectional Engineer, Post Office, Guildford.

The Lineman, Post Office, Guildford.

1	CALL OFFICE - - -	Post Office.
x19	**Chapman,** Lowry, and Puttick, Ltd., Builders, Contractors, Decorators.	Crossways Road.
19	Do. do. -	Oakhurst.
x2	**Coxhead** and Welch, Ironmongers.	Headley Road.
3	**Deas,** F., Grocer - -	Crossways Road.
18	**de Pury** David - - -	Grayshott House.
4	**Grayshott** Steam Laundry Co., General Laundriers.	Grayshott.
5	**Harrison,** R. C., Pharmacist -	Headley Road.
20	**Hill,** E. E., Schoolmaster -	Ling Cottage.
6	**Mitchell** & Co., Butchers -	Headley Road.
7	**Moir,** E. M., School Mistress -	Lingholt, Hindhead.
8	**Morgan-Brown,** J. C., Schoolmaster.	St. Edmund's School.
9	**Munday,** J. & M. A., Fruiterers, Florists.	Headley Road.
10	**Pannell,** C., Boot Depôt -	Crossways Road.
11	**Stokes,** F. A., General Stores	Headley Road.
12	**Vertue,** Mrs. - - -	The Court.
16	**Ward,** J. S., Hotel Proprietor	Glen Lea, Hindhead.
14	**Weston,** Miss A. - - -	Ensleigh.
21	**Whitaker,** A. I. - -	Grayshott Hall.
15	**White,** J. G., Baker and Confectioner.	Homesdale Bakery.
17	**White** Heather Dairy, Dairymen and Confectioners.	Grayshott.
23	**Woods,** E. J., Butcher and Fishmonger.	Headley Street.

* Will be opened shortly.

CHAPTER FOUR

THE NEW CENTURY CALLS.

As the 19th century drew to a close, the area we know as Grayshott had changed dramatically from that of even fifty years earlier. No longer was the heathland and wooded area to the south of Hindhead a sparsely inhabited part of north east Hampshire, with a reputation for lawlessness, and with the small population struggling to eke out a living that was, in many cases, little more than subsistence level. Out of this had emerged a developing and thriving community, which resulted in a growing number of houses, shops, and other buildings, to accommodate the rapidly increasing population.

Whereas in 1872 the population was estimated at only about one hundred souls, just thirty short years later, in the census of 1901, it was shown that there were one hundred and forty three habitable houses and a population totalling six hundred and sixty-six, an amazing increase of over five hundred per cent in less than a generation. Clearly Grayshott was becoming the place in which to live.

Headley Road in 1905

It is significant that a sizeable proportion of the local community consisted of shopkeepers, boarding house keepers and hotel owners and their staff and families. This showed a large and growing "service industry" emphasis, as opposed to other areas and parts of Hampshire, where farming and other agricultural pursuits might still be more dominant.

There were also many summer visitors, from London and elsewhere, drawn to Hindhead, Grayshott, the Devil's Punchbowl and surrounding parts because of the natural beauty and stunning scenery. They came to savour the far-reaching views of gently rolling hills of heathland, with bracken, gorse and wild flowers, all to be enjoyed with invigorating walks in the fresh air for which the area was becoming renowned. In addition, wealthy families were also being attracted to live in this growing area, drawn by the quality of the air with its supposed health-giving properties. Not for nothing was the area known as the "English Switzerland".

By the end of the 1890s there were a total of eleven shops trading in Headley Road, together with another seven in Crossways Road, all serving the local growing community.

If one freezes time in 1895, as an example, we see the following traders pursuing their businesses:

Headley Road:–

Mr Alfred Wells	Forge/smithy
Mr & Mrs Frost	Stationers & barbers
Mr & Mrs Cornish	Grocers
Mr & Mrs Cornish	Drapers
Mrs Hart	Sweet shop
Mr Sayers	Butchers
Mr Moores	Livery & Bait Stables
Mr Inge	Chemists
Mr Charlwood	Saddlers & Boots
Mr Mitchell	Butcher
Mr B Chandler	Livery & Bait Stables
Coxhead's	Ironmongers
Mr Hoy	Fish Shop
(now British Legion)	Boot & Repair shop

Crossways Road:–

Mr Pannell	Boot Shop
Mrs Robinson	General Shop & Post Office
Mr Prince	Bakers
Mr Munday	Greengrocers
Mr Upex	Off Licence
Mr Deas	Grocers
Madame Warr	Stationery & Books
Mr Chapman	Builders Yard

This can only be seen as a snapshot of the village at one moment in time. Over the years to come, the picture would change radically as more shops came and went, some changed hands, and the development of the village continued apace with more houses and shops emerging.

Crossways Road, after 1910

During the 1890s, the churches had yet to be built, and the Fox & Pelican had yet to open its doors for business. Despite this, it was clear that Grayshott was beginning to make its mark locally, and coming into its own as a thriving village community in its own right.

In his book "Hind Head, or the English Switzerland" written in 1898, Thomas Wright described Grayshott as consisting "of a street of new and spruce-looking shops situated near a spot where five roads meet, and a number of handsome private residences and palatial lodging houses dotted about in the remains of a forest of glorious larches and scotch pines. Hind Head, of which Grayshott is only a part, is now one of the most fashionable health resorts within forty miles of London".

"Grayshott looks like a doll's village, not so much because of the size of the houses, but because of their quaintness. The upper storeys are covered with lozenge shaped bright red tiles, made at Haslemere. It has a temporary look, and there is the feeling that one could upset it like a village built with a pack of cards. The tiles, which the damp, south-west winds render necessary, are secured to walls built not of brick but of wood covered with felt. The houses are all new having been erected in the last five or six years. Numbers of persons of distinction reside or have resided at or near Hind Head – famous poets, scientists, novelists, sculptors, journalists, painters. The 'oraculous doctors' never tire of recommending lifegiving Hind Head".

FLORA THOMPSON

One person who came to Grayshott, and was then to make her mark later in the literary world was Flora Thompson (she was Flora Timms at the time), the authoress of "Lark Rise to Candleford" and other books.

She arrived in the village, on foot, on a hot September afternoon in 1898, at the age of twenty, "dressed in a brown beaver hat decorated with two small ostrich tips set upright in front, like a couple of notes of interrogation", to take up the post of assistant in Walter Chapman's village post office in Crossways Road. She was in charge of all the postal and telegraph work there, and was to stay for two years, leaving in September 1900. Walter Chapman was to find his own claim to fame, however, shortly after Flora left, but for very different reasons, as we shall see below.

Taking lodgings in the Post Office at first, she then, a year later, moved to The Ferns, a house in The Avenue, off Headley Road, where she rented a small room for ten shillings a week.

Amongst her many customers were Arthur Conan Doyle, who lived in Undershaw in Hindhead, and George Bernard Shaw, recently married, who lived at Blen Cathra, now St. Edmund's School. They were said to have been keen to use the new-fangled communications system, the telegraph, to keep in touch with friends and colleagues in London and elsewhere. They enjoyed the novelty of being in touch with their friends and literary colleagues in London, via telegraph, and receiving replies and comments the same day.

Flora mentioned later that she had sold them stamps and also handled their telegrams, all the time listening to their conversations in the shop and wishing, as she said "that one of those quick, clever remarks they tossed like coloured balls into the air could have come her way. Perhaps these great examples encouraged my desire to express myself in writing".

Whilst she was serving in the shop "as unregarded as a piece of furniture" none of her customers was aware at the time that they had, in fact, another literary talent living and working amongst themselves, which would later come to fruition and fame.

Self-taught and, for the most part, self-educated, Flora eventually wrote three books which were published, and they were written with much feeling and colour as quiet reminiscences and descriptions of the places where she lived and the characters whom she encountered on the way.

One of her books, which was published posthumously, was called "Heatherley". When she was living in Grayshott, the village was still part of the Parish of "Headley", and it is easy to speculate that her book title might be simply a corruption of the parish name, and that she was referring in her descriptions to life in the village where she had spent a pleasant and formative two years of her early life.

Her most famous work, "Lark Rise to Candleford" has in recent times been immortalised as a television production.

Flora Thompson in 1921

A blue plaque, Crossways Road

DAME AGNES ("AGGIE") WESTON

Aggie Weston devoted most of her life's work among sailors. She was one of the many Victorians who were attracted to the Grayshott and Hindhead area because of the good transport links both to London and to the south coast. The rail links to Portsmouth enabled her to continue her charitable work involving setting up and maintaining a number of Royal Sailors' Rests, or clubs for sailors, by the start of the First World War.

She lived in "Ensleigh" in Crossways Road for seven years, having moved there to be, as she said, "among the pines and within striking distance of Portsmouth" and she dedicated the larger part of her life to her work with the Royal Navy.

Initially, she began to organise recreational facilities for the troops of the Somerset militia, who were temporarily stationed near Portsmouth at the time. When these soldiers left, many for foreign soil, she took pity on them and promised to write to them, to provide a link with home. This task rapidly grew, and eventually this resulted in her starting to publish a newsletter called "Ashore and Afloat", which she continued to write personally until her death. By that time, over 55,000 copies were being distributed.

One of the soldiers, sailing to distant parts on a troop ship at the time, showed a sailor the letter he had received from Agnes and so began her much valued link with the Navy. "We never light our pipes with your letters" a sailor wrote "because you thinks and cares for us".

Her concern with the welfare of her sailors also led her to set up a sailor's rest house in Portsmouth, to give somewhere for the young sailors to stay and relax, rather than roaming the dangerous streets at night. This was a great success, and soon there were Sailor's Rests in all the main naval bases, including several abroad. The Rests were so popular that some local pubs even closed down in the face of the competition, and were then taken over by Agnes to provide even more facilities.

The value of the Rests was recognised by Queen Victoria and she bestowed her patronage and the prefix "Royal" on the Sailor's Rests. The Queen met Agnes on several occasions, and took a close personal interest in her work. She was even given permission to go on board warships of the Royal Navy and "speak freely to the sailors" without being supervised, a privilege denied completely to other civilians, male or female.

She was also well known in Grayshott for bringing parties of sailors from Portsmouth to give concerts in the Village Hall, usually at her own expense, and we saw earlier how she and her men could provide a jolly evening to a packed audience. To the sailors under her wing she was always simply known as "Aggie".

Receiving the honour of being appointed a Dame Grand Cross of the Order of the British Empire (GBE) in June 1918 for her work, she sadly died shortly after in Devonport at the age of seventy-eight, shortly before the end of the First World War. At her funeral, over two thousand officers and men crowded into Western Mill cemetery to pay their respects. She had the distinction of becoming the first woman ever to be given a full ceremonial Royal Navy funeral, an honour given in true recognition of her valuable work.

In 1940 a frigate named HMS "Weston-Super-Mare" very quickly became affectionally known as "Aggie on Horseback". As she herself had said, living her life "among our bluejackets, I wish nothing better than to live and die in such happy service".

Today, a Blue Plaque adorns the front wall of "Ensleigh", unveiled at a ceremony by Mr Brian Deverson, the Executive Director of the Royal Sailor's Rest, the charity started all those years ago by Dame Agnes.

"Aggie" Weston

THE PASSING OF VICTORIA'S AGE.

Queen Victoria died peacefully at Osborne House on the Isle of Wight on the 22nd January 1901, after an epoch-making reign of sixty-four years. The weather on the day of her passing was cold, but dry and with clear wintry skies.

To mark the occasion in Grayshott, a Memorial Service was conducted at St. Luke's, where the Grayshott Brass Band played the "Dead March" three times and also "Rock of Ages" to a packed congregation, with a full choir in attendance. The service was taken by the Curate in Charge, later to be the Vicar of Grayshott, the Rev J.M. Jeakes. The village succumbed to an air of solemnity, in keeping with the sombre mood of the whole country, which lasted for days, until details of the coronation of the new King were announced.

The death of the Queen coincided with a further development in the village. Due to the increase in population, and the growth of the village as a shopping and residential area, it was felt that the time had arrived when Grayshott should seek its own status as an independent ecclesiastical parish, rather than being just part of the Parish of Headley.

In November 1900 the Ecclesiastical Commissioners presented Queen Victoria with a proposed Order for approval of the new Parish. Unfortunately, she died before being able to complete the necessary approval. Because of this, the Order was later signed by King Edward VII, allowing Grayshott to boast that this was the very first Ecclesiastical Order to be signed by the new King. From now on, Grayshott gained its own identity, no longer being just a part of a greater community.

Further events helped to recognise the growth of Grayshott as a place in which to live and work.

Because the village was rapidly developing as both a residential and commercial centre, local people were becoming anxious about health problems, among others, and wanted modern services such as piped water supply, gas and electricity.

Accordingly, in 1901 the village gained its own general electricity supply, courtesy of the Hindhead Electric Light Company. In 1904 the Wey Valley Water Company was given permission by the District Council to lay pipes and supply water to the village, and in 1909 a gas supply was provided by the Haslemere Gas Company. By 1914 a start had been made in providing street lighting.

Shortly after the Village Hall opened, the Parish Magazine was pleased to confirm that "The new Electric Lantern is now in its place in the Village Hall and working admirably. It was first used at the Band of Mercy meeting on Friday October 7th, when an unusually large number of children mustered to hear Mr Stallworthy's 'Stories of Famous Dogs.'"

It is an indication of the growth of a community when we find that clubs, societies and various sports and social groups begin to emerge, and Grayshott was no different. For example, 1897 saw the Band of Mercy being formed to teach kindness to animals by children, Dr. Lyndon was running St. John's Ambulance classes, the Choral Society was in its second year, a Church Lad's Brigade had been formed, and entertainment was also taking place at the Working Men's Club, which also included three one-act plays. The Cricket Club was formed in 1897, the Football Club in 1898, and the Brass Band in 1899. And in January 1901, the Grayshott Hall Rifle Club was formed jointly by the owner of the Hall, Mr Whitaker, together with a very enthusiastic but not very accurate rifle shot, a certain Mr Arthur Conan Doyle.

But as the growth of a village gives rise to friendly social activities, it sadly can also give rise to darker forces, as 1901 showed, with the macabre story of a murder that took place in Crossways Road.

In its issue of 3rd August that year, a local paper reported:

> "The good people of the quiet little village of Grayshott were considerably startled on Monday morning (29th July) by the report that an awful tragedy had been committed in their midst. The news, at first regarded as incredible and impossible, unfortunately proved to be only too true, and great excitement broke out in the village".

Walter Chapman, guilty of murder 1901

The news related to the Postmaster, Walter Gilman Chapman, and his wife, who were known to have an unhappy relationship. They had in fact separated for a period of some months, but had become reconciled, and were living together. On the Monday morning, whilst Mrs Chapman, who had recently given birth to her fifth child, was bathing one of the children, her husband stabbed her to death in a frenzied attack. Soon after, the local constable, PC Merritt, arrived and arrested the forty-five-year-old Chapman, from whence he was taken to Alton, and soon after charged with murder.

At Chapman's subsequent trial at the Assizes at Winchester, Dr. Lyndon gave evidence of the multiple stab wounds that Mrs Chapman had suffered, both to her front and her back, including details of a four-inch length of knife that he had discovered broken off and embedded deep in her back. There was no dispute as to details of the crime, or that Chapman had committed the act, but the Court was only concerned as to whether or not he was mentally unstable at the time.

The judge gave a detailed direction to the jury as to the question of insanity, in law. In turn, the jury took only a very short two hours to find Chapman guilty, but not responsible in law for his actions. Accordingly, he was, as they say, thereafter detained during His Majesty's pleasure, and committed to Broadmoor for the rest of his life.

THE CORONATION OF 1911.

Thursday the 22nd June 1911 saw the Coronation of King George V and his Queen, Mary, in Westminster Abbey. Despite the warm weather of early June, on the 22nd it rained continuously on the day. But this did not dampen enthusiasm, and the village came out in force to celebrate the occasion.

After an early church service, the children of the village assembled at 10 o'clock in the morning and marched to the recreation ground, at the five road junction, where flags were saluted and "Land of Hope and Glory" and the National anthem were sung with gusto, with the Vicar, and Mr Whitaker, as Chairman of the Council, presiding.

"Granny" Robinson plants the tree 1911

Shortly after, Mrs Hannah "Granny" Robinson, who ran her general shop in Crossways Road, and who was representing the old Grayshott, was invited to plant a yew tree there, which she duly did in the presence of a large number of spectators (the tree is still there, alive and well today). The children were then presented with commemorative medals and certificates by Mr Whitaker to mark the occasion.

Beside "Granny" Robinson's tree today

Following this, the crowd adjourned to St. Luke's churchyard, where another yew tree was planted, this time by young Leith Tomkins, nephew of Mrs Whitaker, and Miss Nicolette Simms, and they were said to represent the new Grayshott.

In the afternoon, a large programme of sports was held in a local field, despite the continuous rain causing almost a quagmire in places. The variety of events included a Three-Legged Race, Tug of War, Obstacle Race, Potato Race, Sack Race, Fireman's Race (which had to be abandoned when the participants were called out to an emergency), Musical Chairs Bicycle, Tilting Ring Ladies Bicycle (any ideas? – Ed), Costumes Race (Men), Egg and Spoon Race, as well as the normal sprint and running races.

Musical accompaniment throughout the afternoon was by the Grayshott Brass Band and other local musicians, following which tea was supplied for all in the schoolroom, although it was something of a crush with everybody crowding indoors because of the incessant rain.

By the time the evening had arrived the rain had eased off, and the celebrations were rounded off with a spectacular display of a huge beacon lit on Gibbet Hill in Hindhead, taking its place in the network of beacons that covered the whole of the country at the end of that day, a string of fires being visible for many miles, in tribute to the new King.

Commemorating the 1911 Coronation

And so, the formative period in the growth of Grayshott was coming to an end. In the space of a little over a half century, what had begun as a small collection of dwellings had moved with the times, and reaped the benefit of the forces that were changing the face of the late Victorian period. The start of the twentieth century saw a growing and enthusiastic mixed community, with the development of businesses, housing, residential and leisure, and gaining a maturity that would propel it in the years to come.

But as 1914 beckoned, dark skies were looming over the European continent. Grayshott would be called upon to play its part in the conflict that was to come, and to contribute to the struggle to preserve not only its own future but that of the nation as a whole.

CHAPTER FIVE

GRAYSHOTT AND THE GREAT WAR.

The August Bank Holiday of 1914 was on Monday the 3rd. The weather was fine and warm, although it had been hot and dry for the three months previously, with temperatures frequently in the eighties Fahrenheit.

On that day, for the fourth year running, a gaily decorated refreshment tent was erected on top of Gibbet Hill, organised by the Grayshott branch of the Church of England Temperance Society. The crowds that attended basked in the late summer sunshine, taking in the surrounding glorious heathland countryside with far-reaching views, whilst enjoying refreshments at reasonable prices. The Commons Preservation Society levied a fee of one guinea for the site, which was paid by a local man, Mr HB Dempsey; the tent was staffed by some twelve local helpers, from eleven in the morning until seven that evening, serving soft drinks and light snacks to the visitors.

But at this time of year there was little talk other than of the great European crisis that was developing, which was expected to lead to war. The growing emergency meant that all trains had been cancelled that day, and as few people had motor cars, this meant that visitor numbers were down that year. Despite this, over three hundred people still made the journey to the top of the hill, the last gathering of its kind for several years to come.

The next day, August 4th, at 12.15 pm, Great Britain declared war on Germany. Prime Minister Herbert Asquith's government had given Germany an ultimatum to get out of Belgium by the previous midnight, and its refusal to do so is seen as the trigger for the start of World War One.

In the Grayshott Parish Magazine, the Reverend Simms wrote:

> "It seems at times as if we were dreaming, and that when we wake up all the world will be as it was before… But we are awake, and all else is a dream. We are engaged in the greatest war that history may have to record. Suddenly, countless families have had their hearts focussed behind a veil of secrecy, all preparing to be mourners. Of what the morrow may bring forth we know nothing".

In Grayshott village, the summer outing to Bournemouth, which had been planned for the church choirboys for the 5th August had to be abandoned as all the excursion trains had been cancelled, the Government having restricted all trains to the movement of military personnel and other uses deemed essential.

At High Pitfold Farm in Hindhead, as the local "Herald" reported on the 8th August, a Mounted Gymkhana, which was held every year, similarly could not go ahead as there was now a dearth of horses in the neighbourhood.

As part of the planning for the war that was expected to come any time, the Army, for some time up to now, had put plans in place for the purchase (compulsorily if necessary) of all breeds of horses, which were to be drafted into war service. In the event, horses came to be used extensively during the whole of the Great War, for transport duties, the haulage of guns and wherever motorised transport was not either available or appropriate, in all theatres of war. In all, over the course of the war, Britain was to lose over 484,000 horses, roughly one horse for every two men.

Immediately after the declaration of war, locally, the Army authorities fanned out from Stoughton Barracks in Guildford and proceeded to buy as many horses in the area as they could find. About twenty horses were sent away from around Haslemere on the Tuesday alone.

Householders realised that something had occurred early on the Wednesday, the 5th when the milkman arrived late, explaining that several of his men had been called to the colours, and also that some of his horses, used for pulling the drays, had been purchased by the military.

In Grayshott, Lloyds Bank closed its doors for the whole of that week, in line with all other banks and financial institutions in the country.

At the time when war was declared in August, there was a total of thirteen Grayshott men having enlisted in the armed forces. By the end of December 1914, that number had risen to eighty-nine, an impressive figure that represented over ten per cent of the village's total population. Grayshott was doing "its bit" for the war from the start.

The Rifle Brigade moves up the line

By the end of 1914, both Grayshott School and the Village Hall had been requisitioned for the billeting of troops, when the 7th Kings' Royal Rifles and the 8th Battalion Rifle Brigade arrived in the village for training before departing for war. Both battalions had been formed in Winchester at the start of hostilities, moved to Aldershot, and then transferred to Grayshott from the autumn of 1914 until the following March.

It was noted in the Parish Council Minutes that the agreed charge for billeting the troops was at the rate of 9d per head, sleeping in the School or Village Hall each night. By March 1915, the total income from this source had amounted to £366.17.5d. Some army tents had also been erected on the tennis courts, adjacent to the Village Hall, and this had caused some damage when the ground was churned up and left in something of a sorry state.

Today, a Blue Plaque can be seen above the doors of the Village Hall, as a record of the occupancy by the troops for that period.

The Village Hall plaque

At the same time, a huge military camp was taking shape on nearby Bramshott Common, erected to accommodate the expected large influx of Canadian troops, which rapidly built up as the weeks and months passed. The camp was eventually to boast its own shops, and YMCA, as well as multiple recreation and leisure facilities. It was for many years, and indeed is today still known by many, as "Tin Town" because of the method of construction of many of the buildings. In addition, in nearby Bordon, the whole of the barracks and other buildings in the town were handed over to the Canadian Army.

In Grayshott, the Methodist Church in Headley Road was active throughout the whole war period. It provided teaching accommodation for the pupils of Grayshott School, as well as a canteen and social centre for the troops throughout each week.

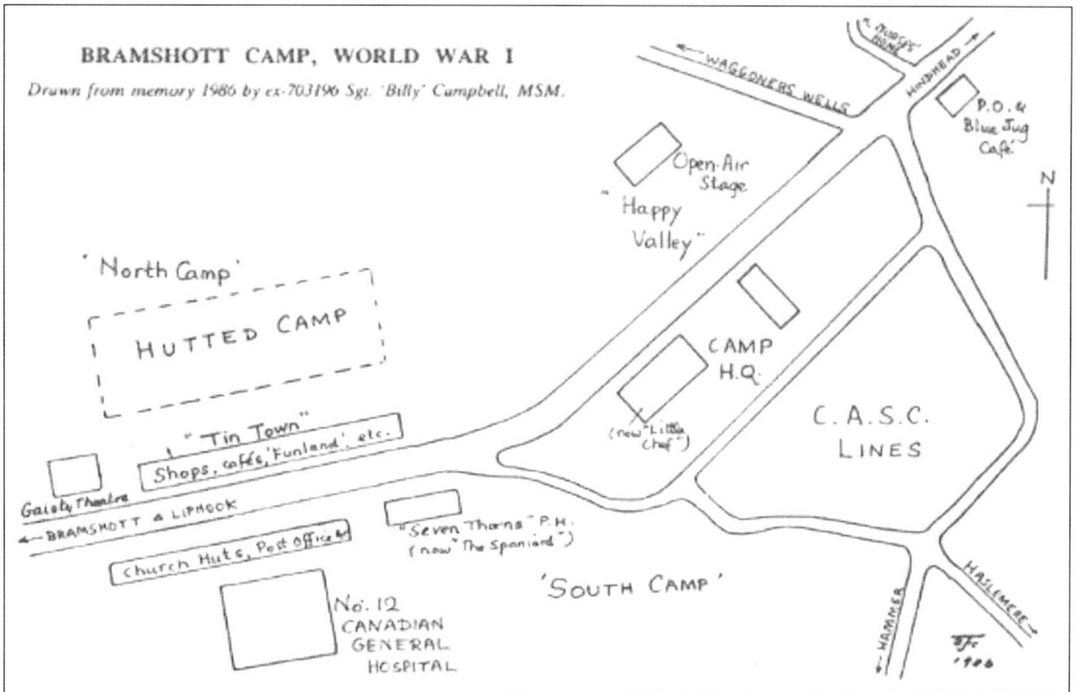

Map courtesy of 'Liphook, Bramshoot and the Canadians" ISBN 0951182900

Bramshott Camp on the A3 – "Tin Town"

Refugees from Belgium began to arrive in the village from October 1914 as part of a huge movement of the population that was fleeing from their own country, following the onslaught of the German advance across the Lowlands of Northern Europe during August and September of 1914. Generally speaking, they were made most welcome locally.

Those arriving were accommodated at various addresses in the village, and the children took their places in the School alongside the local children. According to the school admission registers, there was a total of eleven Belgian children accepted into the school by the end of 1914. Although there is no record that their parents were also resident, it would be reasonable to assume that a number of them also found accommodation in the village.

1914 also saw the opening of the Military Hospital at the Convent of the Cenacle. This became a fully-equipped hospital with twenty-five beds, and served as a section hospital of the Cambridge Military Hospital in Aldershot, for the use of sick and injured serving soldiers. It was ably staffed by the Mother Superior and Sisters, assisted by Dr Lyndon, and his wife Charlotte (she was previously a Sister at Guy's Hospital) as well as local doctors and surgeons, all giving their time and expertise to this most important contribution to the war effort. Mr George Cask, CMG, DSO, the well-known Surgeon to St. Bartholomew's Hospital in London, acted as consulting surgeon.

From the time that it opened, until its closure in January 1919, the Hospital admitted a total of 835 patients to its care, an impressive number given the size of the facility. During that time, casualties were received from all the main battle areas of Europe, together with training accidents and from the Belgian Army in the early days. It certainly helped to relieve the pressure on the Cambridge Military Hospital.

The Military Hospital at "The Cenacle"

Recovering at the Hospital

Grayshott Military Hospital 1914–1919

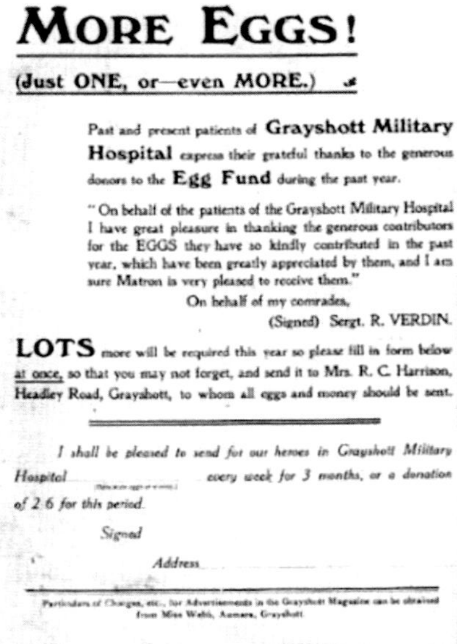

MORE EGGS!

(Just ONE, or—even MORE.)

Past and present patients of **Grayshott Military Hospital** express their grateful thanks to the generous donors to the **Egg Fund** during the past year.

"On behalf of the patients of the Grayshott Military Hospital I have great pleasure in thanking the generous contributors for the EGGS they have so kindly contributed in the past year, which have been greatly appreciated by them, and I am sure Matron is very pleased to receive them."

On behalf of my comrades,

(Signed) Sergt. R. VERDIN.

LOTS more will be required this year so please fill in form below at once, so that you may not forget, and send it to Mrs. R. C. Harrison, Headley Road, Grayshott, to whom all eggs and money should be sent.

I shall be pleased to send for our heroes in Grayshott Military Hospital ________ every week for 3 months, or a donation of 2/6 for this period.

Signed

Address

Particulars of Charges, etc., for Advertisements in the Grayshott Magazine can be obtained from Miss Webb, Aumara, Grayshott.

Announcements were printed in the Grayshott Magazine appealing for the gift of eggs and other provisions that parishioners might be able to spare, and an Egg Fund was specifically run by a local lady, Mrs Harrison, which proved most successful; one particular unnamed supporter in Haslemere made an egg contribution regularly every two weeks.

By the end of 1914, volunteers from Grayshott were serving on ten different ships of the Royal Navy, in far-flung theatres of war all over the world. Men were also serving in the Army in France as well as Egypt, India and elsewhere, not to mention the large number of troops training at home, before being sent to The Front.

Residents were beginning to find life becoming more difficult, with the absence of so many men folk away serving in the military. And it was inevitable that local families would suffer the agony of losing loved ones in the battles being fought.

Before the first year of the war was ended, for example, the Whitaker family mourned the loss of twenty-nine-year-old Captain Harold Whitaker, 2nd Battalion Rifle Brigade. Arriving in France on the 7th November, his unit moved up to the Front, where he was killed by a sniper's bullet only some three weeks later.

He was buried with honour at Fauquissart Military Cemetery in Laventie, France, and today there is a polished bronze plaque to his memory along the side wall of St. Luke's Church.

That same month also saw the death of another local man, Loftus George Levett, who was serving on the armoured cruiser HMS Good Hope. He died when his ship went down off the Pacific coast of Chile, sunk by the German cruiser Scharnhorst, in what was the first major sea engagement of the First World War, today referred to as "The Battle of Coronel". His family lived at "The Ferns" in The Avenue, and was to suffer the loss of two of its sons by the time of peace in 1918.

Another local death was that of Engineer Commander AV Stokes, who went down with his ship HMS Hogue. He was the brother of Miss F. Stokes, who ran the local Post Office at Bramshott Chase.

At home, the church bell of St. Luke's was now rung at midday each day of the week. The purpose of this was to remind everyone of the sacrifices that were being made by soldiers, sailors and airmen everywhere. This gesture was to continue each day throughout the whole of the war period, until the Armistice in November 1918.

By early 1915, the 7th King's Royal Rifles & 8th Battalion Rifle Brigade had left Grayshott for the front, to be replaced by the Oxford & Bucks and the 12th Rifle Brigade. Each Sunday, the troops paraded for the services at St. Luke's, and quickly became familiar sights and sounds around the village; but they too had left Grayshott by the autumn, engaged in heavy fighting in France.

Colonel Maclachlan, of the Rifle Brigade, wrote to the vicar, Reverend Simms, thanking the village for its hospitality, and, in harrowing words, described his men taking part in an action:

> "We had only gone into the trenches that night, and for the next twenty-four hours were fighting for our lives. Practically all the officers are gone, and we lost in killed and wounded about two thirds of the men. We cannot trace a large number of them I fear, as the Germans got the front trenches thanks to using those devilish gases. I am so awfully proud of them, but it is hard to start afresh".

Following the battle, the men of the 8th Rifle Brigade were to receive not less than two Victoria Crosses, two DSOs, 2 Military Crosses and seven Distinguished Service Medals.

In Grayshott, the village did what it could for the war effort. The local League of Honour busied itself by making slippers for French soldiers in hospital, and also knitting hundreds of squares to be made into blankets.

The Grayshott Magazine in March 1915 printed a heartfelt plea:

> "Socks are wanted for the 2nd,10th, 11th and 12th Battalions of the Hampshire Regiment, now serving in France, Salonika and the Mediterranean. All contributions will be thankfully received by the Secretary, Hants and Isle of Wight Military Aid Fund, the Hampshire Depot, Winchester".

Its members also set to work making sandbags, in response to a request received from Lieutenant Crossley, whose troops had been billeted in the village earlier, and who were now serving on the Western Front.

As a result, he wrote to the Reverend Simms in August 1915:

> "We have received five bales of sandbags, all of approximately equal sizes. They are quite all right, and it is most good of you to have made them. Please thank everybody very much indeed. Sandbags are most difficult to get; we have used up a lot here. Two of your bales went to the assist of the building of a vast dugout for a detachment".

Major Bullock, of the same regiment wrote:

> "Ever so many thanks for the sandbags. You do not know how valuable they are, and they are almost unprocurable out here. I hope you are able to keep us supplied. We are most grateful for them".

The Magazine commented:

> "A considerable number of these sandbags have been made by members of the League of Honour. A donation of £5 has been received from Mrs Simms for material, otherwise Mrs Crossley has supplied this. Here is one way of helping in the house".

The murder at Hindhead Chase

Early on in the war, the 9th Canadian Mounted Rifles had arrived at Bramshott and were undergoing training before being sent to France. At the time, their Commanding Officer, and other officers, were billeted with their staff at a house called Hindhead Chase, in Crossways Road.

Sgt. Ozanne, murdered in Grayshott in 1915

This included 22-year-old Assistant Regimental Adjutant Lieutenant George Codere (nicknamed "Fou", or Fool, because of his erratic behaviour). He had been entrusted with the regimental canteen funds, handed over to him by the canteen sergeant, 37-year-old Sergeant Henry Ozanne. Codere took it upon himself to steal most of the funds, and he asked Sergeant Ozanne to help him. Ozanne refused.

Later, Codere invited Ozanne to Hindhead Chase to discuss the matter, and after a brief but heated argument, he brutally killed him with a trench stick (a leather covered rod of lead) and then inflicted a large number of stab wounds on him with a long knife. It was not long before he was discovered, arrested, and taken to Whitehill Police Station.

At his subsequent trial at Winchester Assizes, he was found guilty of murder and sentenced to be hanged, but this was later commuted to life imprisonment on the grounds of his insanity.

Sergeant Ozanne was buried with full military honours in The Mount Cemetery, in Guildford, where his grave can still be seen today.

Since the murder, later occupants of Hindhead Chase have been known to complain about ghostly heavy army boots being heard in the house on occasion, and also that a smell of tobacco smoke was sometimes evident in the house. This has been experienced by several people over the years.

Does Sergeant Ozanne's spirit linger on?

Each year during the war, St. Luke's organised a collection of Christmas parcels to send out to the troops at the Front, and elsewhere, with contributions from parishioners. Each parcel was accompanied by a letter signed by the Vicar. A total of ninety-seven Christmas parcels were sent out in December 1915, following a request for donations from local businesses and schools, plus many personal gifts and household donations.

The case of Private Alfie Bangs

Alfie Bangs was born, and grew up, in the village, in "Woodville", where the family ran, amongst others, a gardening business.

He joined up, in 1906, at the age of eighteen, and served in the 2nd Battalion, East Surrey Regiment. From the start of the war, the regiment was largely posted to areas of the Middle East, where it saw action in what became known as the Mesopotamia Campaigns.

At the end of 1915 he was one of the ninety-seven serving men to whom a Christmas parcel was sent from St. Luke's, containing a pudding and other items, to give creature comfort whilst he was doing his duty with the Battalion.

The parcel went on a long and roundabout journey, travelling as far as India, for nearly a year, before it was eventually returned to St. Luke's, undelivered, but minus the pudding. No explanation was given at the time as to its return.

What no one in Grayshott had known during that time was that Private Bangs had been taken prisoner of war by Turkish troops, following the abject surrender of the eight thousand strong British garrison at Kut-al- Amara in May 1916, in what is now Iraq. The soldiers were marched off into captivity in Turkey, where they were held as prisoners of war in dreadful and insanitary conditions. Of the men who left Kut-al-Amara, a total of 4,250 died either on the way to captivity or in the camps that awaited them at journey's end.

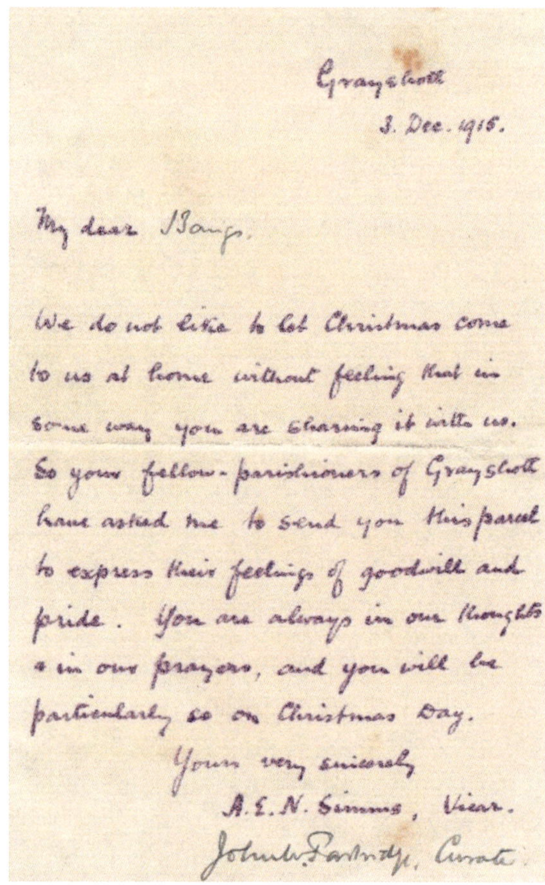

Grayshott
3. Dec. 1915.

My dear Bangs.

We do not like to let Christmas come to us at home without feeling that in some way you are sharing it with us. So your fellow-parishioners of Grayshott have asked me to send you this parcel to express their feelings of goodwill and pride. You are always in our thoughts & in our prayers, and you will be particularly so on Christmas Day.

Yours very sincerely
A.E.N. Simms, Vicar.
John W. Partridge, Curate.

The letter accompanying Private Bang's parcel

Alfie died in the prison camp, but little is known today of his fate. The official records show that he died of disease at Yarbaschi whilst a Prisoner of War, the date of death being recorded as between 1 & 31.8.1916.

The family knew nothing of Alfie's fate at the time, and his death was only confirmed by the Army in May 1919, some six months after the end of hostilities.

From the start of the war in August 1914, there was panic buying in many of the shops as families became increasingly worried about supplies of essential foods. As a result, some shops closed, and hoarding became widespread, despite being officially frowned upon.

The country heavily depended on food imports, bringing in some 80% of wheat, 40% of meat and nearly all sugar from abroad. The Government, although pressed, was reluctant to get involved, or to introduce rationing, as it was felt that it would be better to rely upon market forces and the common sense of people to see things through. This worked tolerably well, but by the summer of 1916 there had been an increase in food prices of 61% from the period July 1914 to July 1916.

As in all parts of the country, Grayshott residents, from children to the elderly, began to feel the effects of the war. There were food shortages, prices were climbing high, and there was an inequality of distribution, with some areas receiving less than they should have expected. Despite this, the idea of rationing was still thought to be alien, and it was felt that a system of voluntary restraint would be sufficient.

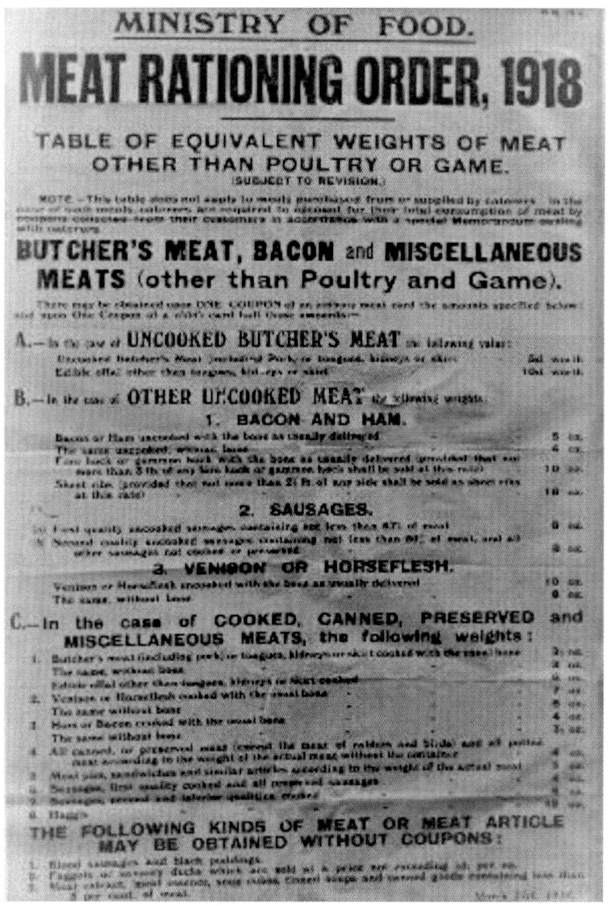

Meat rationing order 1918

By the end of 1916, though, it was becoming apparent that things were getting close to desperate. During that year, the American wheat and potato harvest had suffered failures due to appalling winter weather conditions. In addition to this, during 1916 and 1917 the German submarine menace, which was wreaking havoc on many of the North Sea convoys, finally compelled the government to introduce food controls, although this initially led to voluntary rationing only.

Dramatically, in April 1916, it was announced in the House of Commons that the stock of food for the whole country was down to only three or four weeks' supply. Starvation on a mass scale was on the horizon.

The situation could not carry on, and rationing thereafter became compulsory as from January of 1918. Ration books were issued to each household for butter, lard, sugar and meat, with coupons to be redeemed weekly. And just in case anyone was able to find more than the rationed amount, the Farnham Herald issued a stern warning, saying:

> "Anyone who buys more than his or her immediate requirements is either thoughtlessly or wickedly robbing the poor; and any tradesman who charges one farthing more than is fair is a thief and a traitor to his country".

The Reverend Simms, in his letters to parishioners, encouraged everyone to be strong under the strain of war, to reduce waste, make good use of allotments, and to lend to the cause through investing in the War Savings Association, and also to ignore German propaganda. In November 1917 the King called for a National Day of Prayer, to be held on the 6th January 1918, and thereafter on the first Sunday of each year. Reverend Simms appealed for everyone to help each other with food and fuel, to organise locally the supply of necessities, and to grow as much food as possible.

As with most towns and villages, many Grayshott families had suffered tragic losses of their loved ones. By the start of 1917, for example, the Parish Magazine reported sixteen military dead, of whom thirteen were killed whilst serving in the Army, two in the Royal Navy, and one in the Royal Flying Corps. On top of this there were a further three missing or wounded, as well as four prisoners of war.

During the Great War, multiple deaths within the same family also became a tragedy that was more and more heard of, as the conflict wore on. Five brothers of the Cresswell family of Grayshott were serving, of whom two were to die in battle, three members of the Wood family died, as did three of the sons of the Selwyn family, two of the Voller family, two of the White family, and two of the Levett family. The anguish endured by these, and other families can only be imagined.

By the time of the Armistice in November 1918, the Parish Magazine confirmed a total of thirty-four military deaths in the village, with eight servicemen languishing as prisoners of war, with yet a further one hundred and ten local men still actively serving in all branches of the military throughout the world.

And as if the ravages of war were not enough, by the end of 1918 a deadly influenza epidemic was raging across Europe, and taking its toll on Grayshott residents as well as in the ranks of the military. Bramshott Camp was in quarantine, Grayshott School was closed for three months, and the death toll rose everywhere. In St. Mary's Church, Bramshott, are to be found the graves of 317 Canadian soldiers who perished, and St. Joseph's Roman Catholic Church in Headley Road has 97 Canadian graves. The great majority of these deaths were the result of the epidemic, and largely occurred after the war was officially over.

On Monday 11th November 1918, an Armistice was declared, to mark the end of over four years of hostilities, the ceasefire coming into effect at 11am that day. A service of Thanksgiving was held in St. Luke's to a packed congregation, taken by the Reverend A. Simms, and also in all of the other churches in the Parish.

And in nearby Aldershot, the home of the British Army, a salute of 101 guns was fired, so loud that it was said to have been heard as far away as Winchester.

THE NATIONAL ANTHEM

It is notable that, from August 1914, and throughout the years of the conflict, churchgoers had been reciting the National Anthem in the form of a prayer, spoken quietly and with reverence, on their knees, at each service. From now on, it was once again to be sung, with pride, as a song of praise, standing up.

GRAYSHOTT CLINIC AND THE WAR MEMORIAL

On Friday, 24th January 1919, just five weeks after the Armistice, a meeting was held in Grayshott to discuss ways in which to express the admiration and thanks of the village for the men who had given their lives in the service of their country. A committee was formed, chaired by Mr Ingham Whitaker, with fourteen other members sitting, and it was proposed by Dr. Lyndon that a Cottage Hospital be built in the area, for the benefit of the local community, as well as a separate stone cross War Memorial.

The following October, however, the idea of the Cottage Hospital was dropped after strong opposition was received, and instead it was resolved to build a clinic as a residence for a District Nurse, including a treatment room. The site for the Clinic in School Road was given by Mr Ingram Whitaker and conveyed to trustees on behalf of the Grayshott Nursing Association.

Building work commenced in October 1920. The foundation stone was laid by Mrs Ingham Whitaker, using the same silver trowel that had been used by Catherine I'Anson when laying the foundation stone for St. Luke's Church, and within the Clinic's foundations was lain a fascinating time capsule, which, as we shall later see, was to come to light only a few years ago.

At the same time, work was put in hand for the erection of the new War Memorial. The construction itself was designed by a Mr Clark, the Surveyor of Hereford Cathedral, and modelled on that of the 13th century Clearwell Cross in Gloucester. By early 1921 the memorial was completed, and the dedication service took place on a bright and warm sunny 17th July that year at its then location on the village green. The Commander of Bordon Camp, Colonel-Commandant A C Daly CB, CMG, taking the proceedings, confirmed the dedication, and after a wreath being laid by a Sergeant Alfred Bentley, and prayers said, the Memorial was formally handed over to the care of the Parish Council. This was followed by "The Last Post", sounded by four buglers, plus "Abide with Me", and the laying of further wreaths.

Those commemorated at the time were, and still are today:

Bangs AC	Bridger EJ	Crawte CJ
Cresswell WJ	Cresswell H	Ford A
Hannant C	Halstead GW	Harris G
Hervey GA	Lawrence J	Levett LG
Levett A	Luff L	Miles A
Moore MM	Norman TG	Parker RH
Selwyn AP	Selwyn CW	Selwyn GVC
Slater F	Voller J	Voller J
Whitaker H	White A	White BE
Wood CJ	Wood B	Wood W.

Unveiling the War Memorial, July 17th 1921

Grayshott War Memorial today

The War Memorial did not, however, remain on its original site which was soon thought to be inappropriate. In 1932 it was described as "a dark cross in the middle of a field surrounded by scraps of paper, cigarette boxes and other refuse".

The Parish Council passed a resolution, which resulted in the memorial being moved to its present location just over the road at the junction of Headley Road and Crossways Road. The new site was described in the resolution as being "more fitting and worthy where the beauty and dignity of the monument could be seen".

As for the Clinic, this performed valuable work as a service to the community for many years. In recent years, however, its services, such as the provision of community nursing teams and the child health clinic were moved elsewhere, and with other factors regarding ongoing financial constraints and changes to legislation playing a part, the Clinic was no longer required. As a result, the Clinic building was demolished and a number of houses have been built on the site, as can be seen today.

Grayshott Clinic, from the 1920s

Grayshott Clinic, later, before demolition

CHAPTER SIX

THE MIDDLE YEARS – From 1918 to the 1930s

For the village, the years following the Great War were ones of consolidation, a time when Grayshott cemented the foundations that had been laid in the earlier decades in terms of its place in the wider community. It was now a "place on the map", an attractive village with its own sustained population, a working environment as well as offering a satisfying place in which to live, both to commuters to London and elsewhere, and for those whose living was to be found in the village itself.

For commuters, Haslemere (the nearest station) was just four miles away, and easily reached by a regular service of motor bus. The onward Southern Railway train service to London took just over an hour, without changing. As well as the trains, a regular coach service ran to and from London each day of the week, the return fare being 6 shillings (30p).

Grayshott was gaining a maturity, and this continued, with modest growth, throughout the 1920s and 1930s. As Grayshott became established, there were, in this period, two extensions of the parish boundaries, which had important repercussions in relation to development in future years.

In 1921, an Inquiry was held with a view to regularising the civil parish boundary between Grayshott and Headley, from Whitmore Vale on the north to Headley Road on the south. The effect of this adjustment was to add a total of thirty-five acres, mainly on the Land of Nod Estate, to the village boundaries.

Eleven years later, in April 1932, there was a much more extensive addition to the parish. The wooded Kingswood Firs Estate, adjoining the main A3 road, was added, and this ensured that the attractive residential estate that was to be built there in the future would be part of Grayshott, instead of being just an outpost of the parish of Bramshott.

Having said this, whilst Grayshott enjoyed its modest increase in size, there were also physical constraints on future development, as large areas of land all around the parish came to be owned and managed under the protection of the National Trust, as well as the land remaining in private ownership.

A great deal of land forming Ludshott Common came under the Trust, as did large stretches of Golden Valley, and also the western area of Nutcombe Valley, including "Miss James's Walk". Thus it was that the village was, to a certain extent, contained against the possibility of sprawling development, which in turn was of great value in helping to preserve the village character of Grayshott to this day.

The village in 1920

The village in 1938

PEOPLE NUMBERS

As Grayshott became a settled community, so the population numbers in this period in fact show very little change. This can be indicated as follows:

	1911	*1921*	*1931*
Total	1018	1230	1228

These figures can, further, be broken down to show the numbers of males and female for these years:

Male	491	523	495
Female	527	707	733

What becomes apparent, and indeed striking, is that throughout the inter-war period the figures show a marked higher percentage of females to males. A comparison of the figures above show that the proportion of males to females for the whole of the period was very roughly 40% to 60% in favour of females, i.e. at any one time there were about one third more women than men in the village. This cannot be attributed entirely to the effect of the First World War, as the first statistics are from 1911, i.e. before the war, although it must be the case that the effect of war deaths, as well as population movement caused by the war, was an influencing factor. There is indeed an enigma here, and one that might bear further investigation.

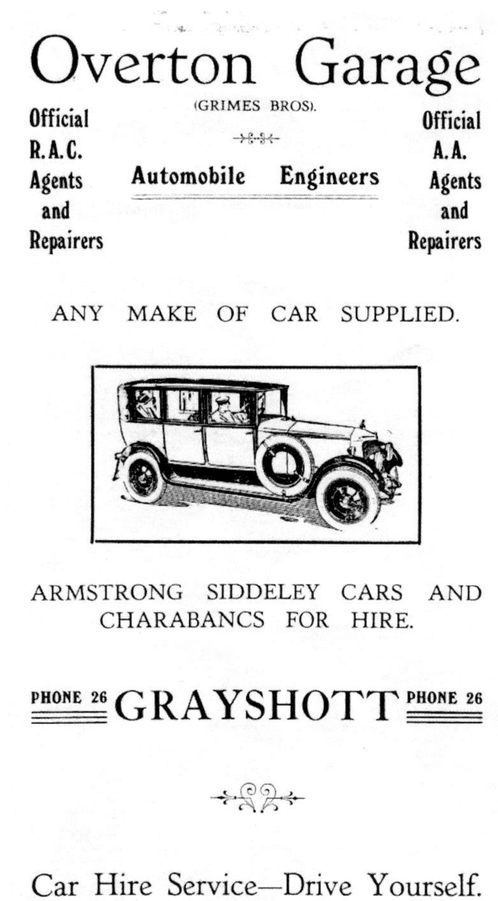

Thriving Village business in the 1920s

In Britain as a whole, we find that, in the 1920s and beyond, the size of the average family was smaller than in the Victorian era, with families of three or four children now being most common. The incidences of infant mortality had become far less prevalent, due to the rapid increases in medical knowledge and expertise, partly fuelled by the medical urgencies that had prevailed during the previous years of war.

In the field of education, in 1900 it was quite common for children to leave school when they were only 12 years old, and then go out to find work in order to help feed the family. In 1921, however, the Education Act raised the school leaving age to 14. Also, state primary education was now free for all children, and started at the age of five years. In Grayshott, the village School continued with increased numbers of pupils, despite the fact that it was handicapped by a shortage of staff. The Headmaster Mr A E Bott resigned in 1919, and his successor, Mr W T Varley, found it difficult to manage, having to rely upon temporary teaching staff and supply teachers for prolonged periods.

In terms of private families living in the village, in 1911 there were 226 in total, and this rose modestly to 264 after ten years (1921), and to 303 ten years later, in 1931.

And in order to accommodate the rising population, the number of houses built was growing, albeit at a controlled pace. During the 1920s and 1930s, there was a massive, mostly suburban, house building programme under way in all parts of the United Kingdom. Partly encouraged as a means of recovering from the Depression of the early 1930s, virtually all towns today, and many villages, contain streets and estates that display the building fashions of the age, often with bow windows and lines of semi-detached houses.

A number of attractive individual houses were built along the unmade and unadopted road running from Glen Road to Whitmore Vale Road by the early 1920s, which became known as "Church Lane". Also, 1921 saw the first of a number of Council cottages being built in Beech Hanger Road. In addition, there was a certain amount of development in Crossways Road and Headley Road, although these two roads were to see a far greater amount of construction work after the end of the Second World War.

One of the only "developments" of note at the time was that of the houses in Tarn Road, where eight houses were built by the year 1938, although this is, of course, strictly speaking in Surrey rather than Hampshire.

"THE GRAYSHOTT ESTATE"

There was one large proposed development, which never came to fruition. In the late 1920s, the Grayshott Hall Estate changed hands, the new owner being Mr Horace Wright. Following his purchase, an ambitious plan was proposed which would have seen the development of over two hundred houses, located to the west of the village, including what is now Applegarth, in the east to the bottom of Whitmore Vale and along Whitmore Hanger, both sides of Hammer Lane and west as far as the north side of Headley Road opposite Ludshott Common.

If the plan was to go ahead, there was concern within the Parish Council that, in effect, about up to half the total acreage in the parish could change hands. There was much deliberation, with resolutions passed requesting further information and detail.

In the end, the plan for development was dropped, and the worst fears of overdevelopment were not realised, possibly because the developers lost interest at the time. The only construction that eventually took place was confined to the Kiln Way and Fir Way areas, to the west of the parish, and it was not until the 1970s that a completely separate scheme came to fruition, when planning permission was eventually granted for the development of the Waggoners Estate, as we know it today.

ROADS & STREET LAMPS

As Grayshott grew and settled in the 1920s, so the question of the state of the roads came more to the fore. There was increased traffic on the unmade roads, as motor cars and other vehicles became popular, together with more pedestrians, just at a time when it was apparent that there was no clear policy or local authority arrangement for the maintenance or repair of the village highways.

Any maintenance was on a more or less ad-hoc basis, quite often undertaken by shopkeepers and adjoining householders wanting to keep their particular stretch of pavement and road in good order. But during severe weather, for example, this became something of an unwanted obligation, and the roads, particularly in winter, could become difficult to navigate, if not sometimes outright dangerous.

For example, during one particularly snowy period in March 1927, the Parish Council minutes noted that "Mrs Kirkness said her housemaid went out on her bicycle and had to be brought back on a lorry". History does not record what happened to the lady, but it is clear there were concerns about the inadequate and piecemeal clearance of snow at the time.

In 1930, Hampshire County Council formally took over the maintenance of all classified roads in the county, a move welcomed by most residents. However, this did give rise to some protests when the Council started to put in kerbing in Headley Road, as many people felt that this was having the result of reducing the pavement widths.

At the same time, there were increasing complaints about vehicles speeding through the village at all times of the day and night, especially motor bikes and small buses. As a result, 30-mile-an-hour speed limit signs began to appear in the late 1920s. This in turn came to be introduced in all built up areas in Britain in 1934.

Another road hazard at the time can be put down to street lighting, either inadequate or totally absent, as well as an absence of roadside footpaths. This caused a number of incidents over the years. For example, in January 1938, it was noted that five women returning from Christmas Eve Midnight Mass at St. Joseph's had fallen into a ditch on the south side of Headley Road, with the result of three sprained ankles," and Major Wessel had to drive them home." Major PT Wessel was the Chairman of the Parish Council at the time, in the role until 1944.

Street lighting started to appear in this period, to the extent that in October 1926 there were eight street lamps in the village, rising to fourteen in 1935, and twenty-seven by 1938.

Henry Robinson's shop in Crossways Road 1928.
"Granny" Robinson is seen here with her family
along with Fred Aslett, the local Wall's Ice Cream man

"Woods" butchers, Headley Road

Grayshott Bus outside the Fox & Pelican

Headley Road circa 1926

The Five Crossroads 1920s

DEPARTURES

In the New Year of 1928, Mr and Mrs Ingham Whitaker left Grayshott following the sale of their home, Grayshott Hall to a Mr Horace Wright. Their departure was felt keenly in the village, as the family had done so much over the decades to promote the development and growth of Grayshott and its institutions and services.

The Rev Garth Ireland, writing in the Grayshott Magazine in November 1927, said that "a sadness was cast over Grayshott when the news came that (they) were leaving the Hall. It is difficult to imagine Grayshott without them, and there is a feeling of very real sorrow that this change must be made. How we all wish it were in our power to prevent it!"

The ownership of Grayshott Hall was to change a number of times over the years to follow. The building did not change much as a result, but it is fair to say that its place in forming a prominent part in the life of the village was to lessen as a result. It still has a significance, of course, as a current health spa, but with a different public emphasis.

C. BRIDGER & SONS, F.A.I.,
HINDHEAD and HASLEMERE.

ONE OF THE CHOICEST ESTATES IN THE HOME COUNTIES.

In the midst of the beautiful Pine and Heather Country. Unrivalled situation. Magnificent Southern Views. Practically surrounded by National Trust Commons.
Golf at Hindhead and Liphook within easy reach. Haslemere Station 5 miles.

"GRAYSHOTT HALL," NEAR HINDHEAD.

THE STATELY MANSION IS OF ATTRACTIVE DESIGN,
beautifully proportioned and perfectly appointed. It contains
MAGNIFICENT LOUNGE HALL. BILLIARD ROOM. 4 FINE RECEPTION ROOMS. COMPLETE OFFICES
14 PRINCIPAL BED ROOMS. 7 BATH ROOMS. STAFF BED ROOMS.

Co.'s Electric Light, Power, Gas and Water installed. Modern Drainage. Central Heating. Telephones.
Excellent Lodge. Garages for 6. Stabling for 9. Chauffeur's Flat. Farmery with Bailiff's house. 2 Cottages.

EXQUISITE GARDENS OF GREAT BEAUTY. BEAUTIFUL WOODLANDS.
3 TENNIS COURTS (1 HARD). 30 ACRES OF PASTURE LAND.

85 ACRES IN ALL.

A REALLY OUTSTANDING ESTATE OF GREAT CHARM.

HIGHLY RECOMMENDED from personal inspection by the SOLE AGENTS :—
Messrs. C. BRIDGER and SONS, HINDHEAD (Tel. 65), and HASLEMERE (Tel. 4).

Grayshott Hall for sale 1927

Having left the village, Alexander Ingham Whitaker moved to an address in London, and died in Belgium in 1933 at the age of seventy-six. He was buried at St. Luke's on September 3rd that year. It was said at his funeral:

> "Grayshott has been singularly fortunate in having the Whitaker family to do all the generous things that have been done for the village. We honour Mr Whitaker's memory and his name will live long in our parish".

Another character intimately connected with the early history and formative years of Grayshott was Mrs Hannah "Granny" Robinson, who died in 1929 at the age of 93 and was buried at St. Luke's on November 18th.

She had been a well-known figure in the village for many years. With her husband, Henry, she was responsible for keeping a shop in the early 1870s at "Mount Cottage", on the Headley Road, and then, later, opening the first shop to be established in Crossways Road in 1887, selling all general goods, groceries, sweets and much else. Her grave can be found in the churchyard of St. Luke's today.

THE SILVER JUBILEE OF 1935

The village celebrated the Silver Jubilee of King George V and Queen Mary in 1935, on Monday the 6th May, being 25 years from the actual day of the Coronation, with much gusto and enthusiasm.

Early in the morning, there was a dedication of flags in St Luke's Church, followed by a Service of Thanksgiving, and with much ringing of the church bells, which pealed out at length. In the afternoon, there was a very full gathering of sports events on Phillips Field, where the large crowds were noisily entertained by several local bands. The weather was fine and sunny, and it seemed as though almost the whole village had turned out for the event.

This was followed later in the afternoon by tea being served in the Village Hall, where several forms of entertainment were put on, mainly for the benefit of the children, as well as a popularly attended dance. The Fox and Pelican provided a wonderful and varied supper for pensioners, at the cost of 2s.6d a head, and Jubilee Mugs were widely distributed.

The busy day was rounded off with a huge bonfire which was lit on Gibbet Hill. This was attended by several hundred people, and was one of a line of fires seen to be marching across the Hampshire and Surrey countryside, and beyond, in celebration.

The Grayshott Girl Guides contributed to the occasion by planting a Hawthorn tree, still to be found by St. Luke's Church, on the five crossroads. The tree and the railings were, originally, funded by the Grayshott Mothers Union. The railings were restored in 2012 to mark the Diamond Jubilee of our Queen today.

After all expenses were paid for the Jubilee celebrations, there was a surplus of twenty-five pounds in hand, and this was used to improve the front of the Village Hall, with the erection of a stone and brick wall with four piers connected by a wrought iron chain. This is still there to this day.

SOCIAL LIFE AND SPORTS

The social life of the village thrived during this period. The Dramatic Society was popular for some years after the Great War, with many presentations and meetings in the Village Hall, as was the growth of the Women's Institute. The W.I. had been formed in Grayshott in December 1925, and continued for many years as a popular and influential meeting format for the ladies of the village, encouraging and teaching many areas of craft work, cooking and other household interests.

The Village Hall Men's Club was very active, also the Working Men's Club, and, in 1932, the British Legion Club, as well as the Grayshott Bowling Club, which used the land to the side of the Village Hall now occupied by the Fire Station. For sports, the new tennis courts and the playing fields were used extensively by such associations as the Tennis, Football and Cricket Clubs, hosting such events as the I'Anson Competition Cricket Cup and the Miller Cup, for mid-week teams on early closing days. Other associations followed over the years, and all served to demonstrate that Grayshott was now a popular and contented place in which to live and play.

As the 1920s and 1930s progressed, Grayshott continued to show a growing and deepening maturity, as a community that had shown extraordinary development in the space of less than a century. The village had been born out of the growing popularity of the local area of countryside in order to service the needs of those coming not only to visit the region, but also to lay down their own roots. The resulting outcome of such development was that of a settled community with its own identity nestling on the North East Hampshire/Surrey border.

In those years, the village had settled its own parish boundaries, distinct from its neighbours, and in the same period the population had more than doubled from that at the turn of the century.

The village had also acquired the usual trappings which give the flavour of village life, such as its own public house, churches (and more than one), a large village hall, supporting a plethora of clubs and social activities, many and varied shops, and its own Parish Council.

Public utilities had also been laid in earlier years, such as electricity (Hindhead Electric Light Company from 1901), mains water (Wey Valley Water Company from 1904), gas (Haslemere Gas Company from 1909), and street lighting was also starting to reach the village from 1914 onwards. On top of this, various pieces of land had been given to the village over the years, by way of allotments, playing fields, a village green, and so on.

By any standard, Grayshott could be seen as a community that had come into its own as the years passed by.

By the end of the 1930s, in Britain as a whole, the dark days of Depression and unemployment from the early 1930s were now largely a memory. Unemployment continued to fall as the years passed and by 1938 it was around ten per cent of the working population. For most people with a job, living standards in that period rose considerably.

In the home, new styles of furniture and architecture appeared, such as the fashion for Art Deco, with its geometric and more rigid lines and shapes. Also, new innovations were becoming popular, with many homes enjoying the ownership of such items as vacuum cleaners, washing machines, and electric ovens. By 1939, there were about a million and a half electric ovens in Britain, together with about nine million gas ones.

And home ownership became more common. Whereas in 1900 about 90% of the population rented their homes, by the end of the 1930s, more than 27% of homes had become owner occupied, many with more than one bedroom, and with inside toilets.

Food was cheaper, more plentiful, and fresher than before the First World War. Hygiene in food shops was much better, and fruit was virtually available the whole year round. More and more people were now eating tinned as well as packaged foods.

Butchers were now starting to keep their meat in refrigerators, and, for the first time, frozen foods were becoming available, the process having been perfected by Mr Clarence Birdseye in America in the late 1920s. This first became available in Britain in 1937, marketed by Smedleys.

In the home, most families still sat down together to meals at set times of the day. Lunch was an important meal, often the main meal of the day, with tea following in the early evening, after the father had returned from work. For many middle-class families, this would then be followed by supper later in the day.

However, dark storm clouds were once again gathering over the European continent, as they had just over two decades earlier. After the Munich Agreement of 1938, it became more and more apparent that another war was becoming imminent, and that the village would have to brace itself for a further conflict of huge proportions.

From the spring of 1938 onwards, for example, Major Wessel took a leading role as the village started to take steps to recruit local men for training in connection with air raid precautions, as the world gradually prepared to put itself onto a war footing once again.

CHAPTER SEVEN

THE HOME FRONT, 1939–1945

The talk of war had been on everyone's lips in the months before September 1939. The slide towards conflict was something that nearly everyone had lived with, and most people believed that war was the most probable outcome of the events that were taking place throughout Europe at the time.

When people gathered round their radio sets on that fateful Sunday morning of 3rd September at 11.15am and listened to the Prime Minister, Neville Chamberlain, make his speech, cracking with strain, stating that "this country is at war with Germany", it came as no great surprise to most people.

In fact, the Government had already been putting civil defence measures and other preparations in place for some years prior. As part of this, for example, 1937 saw the Air Raid Precautions Act being passed, when all local authorities were required to make detailed plans for dealing with air attacks.

In Farnham, for example, the Town Council in early 1939 had converted the Town Hall to a control room, with staff nominated as officers in charge, two plotting officers and clerks, message supervisors, women telephonists and numerous dispatch riders. The tables, the maps, the plotting flags, and the switchboard plugs were all in place. The town was ready for whatever came.

The MP for Farnham, Sir Godfrey Nicholson, gave a stirring speech at Frimley Warren, declaring that Britain was prepared for any eventuality.

The year 1938 saw the Auxiliary Fire Service (AFS) being formed, and also the Women's Voluntary Service (WVS). In the months prior to the start of the war, many hundreds of thousands of men and women had volunteered to join the Reserves of the various branches of the armed services, and the Government started to produce many public information leaflets, covering such topics as air raids, the need for black-outs, and warnings on possible gas attacks.

With the issue of gas masks, the government was well prepared – thirty-eight million of them had already been issued by the outbreak of war.

Everyone was being encouraged to volunteer for some form of war work. The government produced the National Service Handbook, containing a catalogue of the activities for which people could volunteer, such as Air Raid Wardens, Ambulance drivers, Territorial Army, Police War Reserve and so on. By the time of the outbreak of war, some two and a half million people had been enrolled in one form of civil defence or another, as wardens, fire fighters, rescue workers and in many other capacities.

As part of the precautions being taken, the government began preparing for air raids. By 1939 there was an air raid precautions system already in place, with barrage balloons and air raid sirens. People were encouraged to obtain Anderson shelters (those on lower incomes could get them free) which could be dug into their gardens and covered with earth. Later on, people without gardens could obtain a Morrison shelter, which was a steel cage that you erected indoors, in order to find some protection from bombs.

In July 1939, Surrey and Hampshire took part in a practise blackout over the Saturday night of the 8th and Sunday morning of the 9th. The whole area heard the air-raid sirens going off at regular intervals, followed by the 'All Clear'. Street lamps, pedestrian crossing beacons and the like were covered with sacks, motorists could only drive with their side lights on, and then deflected away from the sky as well, and householders had to screen their windows, with no lights visible from the sky. The following month, a similar exercise took part, and the public was warned of severe penalties that would follow if the practise was not followed.

Rationing in the country began in September 1939, when petrol was rationed. As the war continued, rationing was to become much more stringent and widespread. In January 1940 butter, sugar, bacon and ham were rationed. Tea was rationed from July 1940, and from March 1941 jam and marmalade were rationed. This was followed by cheese rationing in May 1941, and later in that year, eggs and milk as well.

When war was declared on 3rd September 1939, it was already in many peoples' minds that the Germans would bomb British cities, causing great loss of life. Because of this a great movement of evacuation took place, with children being moved from the cities to the countryside. Altogether, some 827,000 children of school age, plus 103,000 teachers and helpers, left the major cities of Britain. A further 524,000 children under school age and their mothers and helpers also left, plus 13,000 pregnant women and 70,000 disabled people. However, most of the evacuees were to return home within a few weeks or months of the start of war, when the expected bombing campaign did not materialise.

In Grayshott, the Infant School reopened on Monday, September 11th after the summer holidays. One of the first effects of the war was felt when, after the declaration, a large number of children evacuated from London and other populated areas, came to stay in the district.

Due to its proximity to Aldershot and other army camps, Grayshott was not designated as an evacuation area for civilians, as it was officially described as being in a "Military Zone". This meant that child evacuees were not compulsorily billeted on local families. But this did not prevent concerned parents and relatives from sending their children away from what they perceived to be danger areas, such as city centres, ports and docks.

Because of this, the School saw an extra thirty-five children being admitted that autumn 1939 term, out of a total of one hundred and fifty-seven pupils, an increase of some twenty per cent over the previous term. At one time in 1941 there were eighty-seven evacuee children from London and Portsmouth attending the school as a direct result of the Blitz and other terror bombing raids and firestorms in the cities; this, when the numbers were added to those of the local children, meant that the school building was struggling to cope with the increase. Among other measures taken, this led to some pupils being transferred to an overspill of classes in the Village Hall.

The village began to take on the looks of a community at war. All the street lamps were covered, and houses became subject to the black-out, which was rigidly enforced by the local ARP Warden, who had charge of the ARP hut located at the bottom of Headley Road in what is now the estate agent's office of Messrs. Peter Leete and Partners. The hut was equipped with a full emergency switchboard, as well as a good supply of gas masks, fire extinguishers and stirrup pumps. Air Raid sirens were located at the Fire Station, and these were to become a familiar sound, to be followed later by the All Clear.

The ARP Station 1939–1945

One of the effects of the black-out was that, from November 1939, the school's times for opening were changed, to enable children having a distance to go, to reach home before dark. School now finished every day at 3.15pm, and not an hour later. Also, three rooms in the school building had their windows painted over as a protection against flying splinters in air raids, and the children had frequent practices of air raid and fire drills. At the same time, the Government made it known that there was a real possibility of highly poisonous gases being dropped on towns and villages by the German Luftwaffe, and accordingly everyone was issued with a gas mask, including babies and children.

Gas masks (affectionately known as "snouts") had to be carried at all times, and were kept in a cardboard box with a strap made of string. One ex-pupil recalls of the gas masks "they smelt strongly of rubber, steamed up, you could not see, and were very tight fitting. It was a great joy when we were able to take them off".

She continued "We had to plant potatoes in the fields at the Land of Nod in May and then pick up the potatoes in October, and we were given a week off school for each. When the rose hips were ripe in the hedgerows, these were collected and taken to school to be sent away to be made into rose hip syrup. Mrs Crudgington, the school cook, made the school dinners, dried eggs being used as one of the ingredients. School dinners were eaten by all the children as food rationing was in force. There was no choice, "you either ate it or went hungry".

During 1940 and 1941 there were frequent air battles in the skies over Grayshott, and there were many Air Raid warnings at the time. The Battle of Britain is generally taken to have started in July 1940 and ended on October 31st. The main area of battle was over the Kent skies, but the aerial combats often moved to the skies over Surrey and Hampshire. As the battle progressed during the summer, the blue skies above the village were crisscrossed with lines of contrails as the fighter planes fought their deadly battles.

This was followed in 1941 and thereafter by the sound of frequent bomber formations flying over, on their way to London and other target cities. People still have memories of lying in bed at night and hearing wave after wave of aircraft droning overhead, on the way to their targets, as Grayshott was under the flightpath of many such sorties. Later at night, the bombers would return, often more raggedly, perhaps off-loading the occasional unused bomb, although there were no direct hits on the village.

Graham Yarborough, living at the family's business "Yarboroughs" fish game & poultry shop in Headley Road recalls that:

> "Our business premises had a large cellar. In the 1940s local residents came down to this cellar before they became blasé about the raids. On one occasion my father went up to look about. He saw a huge circle of German bombers seeming about four feet abreast with just five RAF fighters diving in and out of them and firing away. Suddenly there was a banging on the side wall and everyone dived for cover; it was a line of fired Browning machine gun bullets which had missed the target (and hit our wall)".
>
> "There were many aerial combats to be seen over the local skies and a number of German planes came down both in Hindhead, in Golden Valley, and the surrounding areas. In March 1941 there were very few nights that German raiders were not over our area. Also, Portsmouth came under awful bombing raids, and one could see from upstairs the changing red glow in the sky, and sometimes distant rumbles, even with the South Downs in between".

THE HOME GUARD

By May 1940, it was feared by most people that a German invasion was imminent. As a result, the Government's War Secretary, Mr Anthony Eden, called upon all men between the ages of seventeen and sixty-five "not presently engaged in military service" to become Local Defence Volunteers, to provide a "home guard" against invasion. By July 1940, when the LDF came under the authority of democratically elected officers, the new Prime Minister, Winston Churchill, referred to them in one of his speeches as the Home Guard, and the name stuck. Occasionally they were also known as the "Parashots" but, whatever the name, it was the first citizen's army to be formed in Britain since the threat of a French Napoleonic invasion way back in 1803.

The village had its own Grayshott Home Guard, designated No.15 Company, Platoon 15, D Company, 24th Hampshire Home Guard, the headquarters of the 24th being in nearby Alton. It was commanded by a local schoolmaster and retired member of the Northumberland Fusiliers, Captain John William Slater, who had won a DCM in the trenches of France in the autumn of 1915. It was said that he attended all Home Guard meetings accompanied by his two Whippets.

The Home Guard had 4 distinct duties, which were to:

a. report any information of importance that might relate to enemy movements or infiltration.

b. delay and obstruct the advancing enemy for as long as possible.

c. protect vital points, such as railways, telephone exchanges etc.

d. act as guides for the regular Army.

The Home Guard drilling 1940

Training consisted of drills in the Village Hall and elsewhere, with weapons training, first aid, and use of gas masks among the many topics needed to prepare the country, to be on guard at all times in case of invasion.

On the corner of the junction of Headley Road and Crossways Road was a wooden post with a Bren gun mounting on top. The gun was always seen to be facing down Crossways Road, towards the Portsmouth Road. When enquiring why it was facing this particular direction, the answer was always given that the invading Germans would, of course, come up from Portsmouth.

Some years after the war, Captain Slater related two amusing incidents from his days in the Grayshott Home Guard.

In one, some young regular soldiers and their older officers from the Royal Sussex Young Soldiers Regiment came to train the Platoon, as they considered that the Grayshott Home Guard was using out-of-date methods and needed to learn some proper up-to-date soldiering. Following this training, a night exercise took place using the techniques and experience gained in the training.

It was the intention that the Home Guard Platoon should try and capture the Sussex Regiment headquarters, which was located in the wooded area of Kingswood Firs. However, with cunning diversions, the Platoon gave the impression they were about to attack one side of the headquarters, which caused the Sussex defenders to lower their guard on the other side. The Grayshott Platoon then doubled back smartly, keeping under cover, and captured the headquarters from the other side. In doing this, there was apparently one mighty scrap, and Capt. Slater lost his helmet in the fight but managed to save his pride. Victory to the Grayshott Platoon.

There was also the story of "milking the bull" belonging to a local farmer, a Mr Baird. One of the younger and less experienced members of the Platoon was persuaded by his fellow soldiers to go and milk "the cow". Shortly after, he returned, white-faced and terrified, but fortunately unharmed, as the bull was of a gentle persuasion. He had learned a very rapid lesson in bovine anatomy.

The Home Guard was a constant presence in the village, in marching formations as well as taking part in exercises and practise encounters with the enemy. Happily, it was not to see any action and, as with other units, was disbanded at the end of 1944.

THE ARMY & THE CAMPS

Grayshott was literally surrounded by the military, from the long-established sprawling camps at Aldershot on one side, to the more recent camps that grew and flourished at Headley, Woolmer Forest, Bramshott, Ludshott Common and elsewhere, as well as the huge army presence at Bordon.

Canadian sappers completed the camps at Ludshott and in addition, at Bramshott, a six hundred bed hospital was taken over, upgraded and made ready for the casualties of war that were expected, on the site of the old World War One hospital there. Also, a Canadian Light Anti-Aircraft unit was set up, amongst many other preparations that were completed.

On the outskirts of Grayshott, on the site of what is now the Waggoners Estate, a searchlight unit was set up and put into operation. This was located in what was then a wild hay meadow opposite Grayshott House, and comprised the searchlight itself, a defensive light machine gun emplacement, and a number of concrete huts, accommodating the crew of nine men.

A section of the 63rd Searchlight Regiment, Royal Artillery, this formed part of a lengthy co-ordinated chain of searchlights across the whole of Southern England as an answer and a deterrent to the frequent bombing raids that were taking place. Although long since developed for housing, the site is still known by many today as "The Searchlight Field".

Searchlight unit in action

Ludshott Common came to be used as a huge tank training ground. All varieties of tanks and heavy military machinery were driven and tested throughout the war, centred on the Canadian Camp Superior remnants of which can still be found today. As a result of this, the Common became little better than a sea of mud, completely bare of vegetation. It was said that "It was the tanks and the lorries and what not, going forwards and backwards, that killed the heather and everything; it was just like a rice field – churned up the entire common – no vegetation left at all". Local resident Jane Durham recalls that large sections of the common were polluted with oil.

In Grayshott itself, the Canadians were a common sight, and were by and large very friendly and welcomed. It was recalled that they were generous with sweets, chocolate and 'gum' for the children and with gifts of cigarettes and food to families where they visited, civilian rationing being severe at the time. Each Christmas, the children at Grayshott school were treated to a party given by the local Canadian units.

Canadian troops waiting for the day

The school log for 23rd December 1942 states "School was closed at 12 o'clock today in order to allow the children to attend a party given by the Canadian Military Authorities".

The children would be collected up by military lorries, and taken to Camp Superior for the parties, where Father Christmas would arrive on a bren gun carrier, handing out sweets. They were given presents, and enjoyed film shows, and as much as they could to eat. A rare treat indeed, for children growing up knowing of little other than rationed meals.

And in the Village Hall, Grayshott villagers ran dances for the troops, which were very popular and gave rise to many friendships that blossomed at the time.

In the village, the biggest effect was the build up of army traffic, especially as late 1943 turned into 1944. Army vehicle parks built up slowly, as the roads became full with an endless procession of lorries, tanks, armoured cars, staff cars and jeeps, as well as huge landing craft known as "Ducks" (DUKWs). At times it was difficult to cross the roads, which were themselves churned up with lines of caterpillar tread-marks, which, it is said, were still visible for years afterwards.

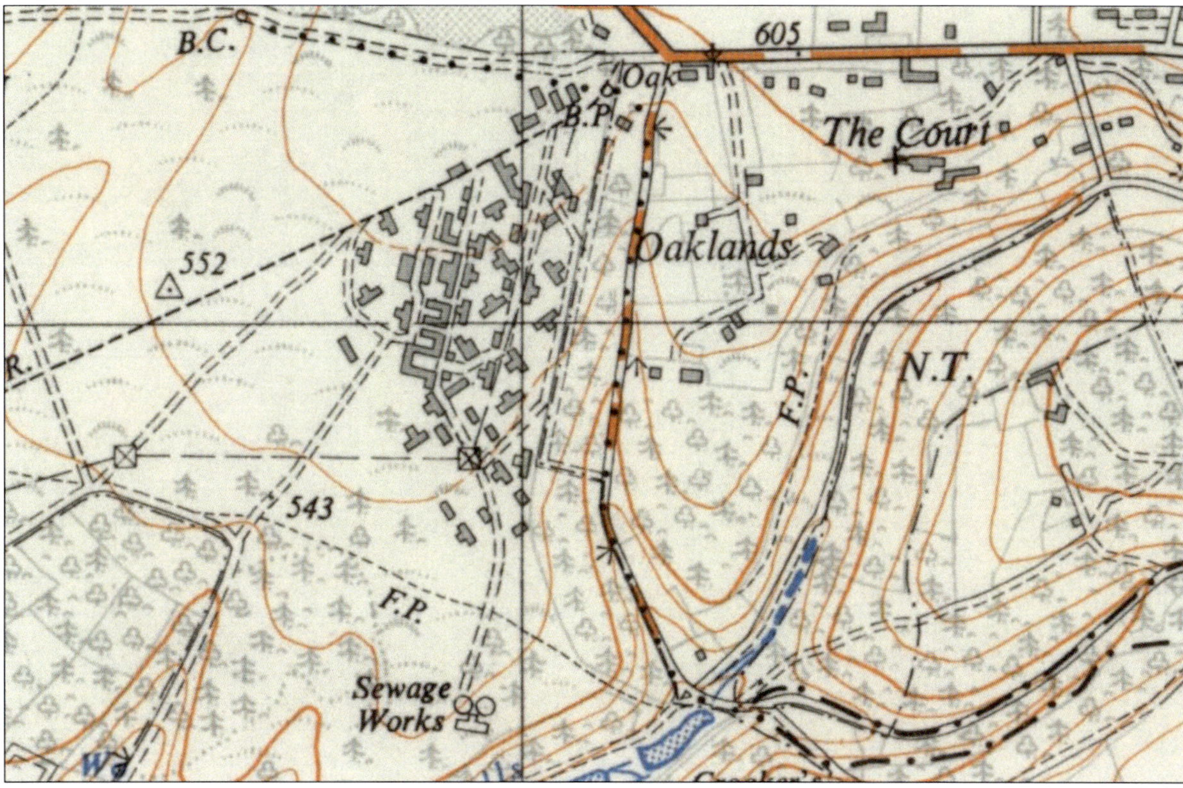

Superior Camp on Ludshott Common

It felt as though there were heavy military vehicles everywhere, and it became commonplace to see small tented camps springing up overnight at points along all the main roads. The Parish Council received frequent complaints from villagers about the state of the roads, which were heavily damaged in places, due to the army traffic, but to little effect at the time.

This lasted, of course, until the start of the D-Day landings in early June 1944, when, almost overnight, it seemed as though nearly all the troops had gone, although the camps in the area were still very much part of local life, for months yet to come.

COMING DOWNS

There were a number of incidents where aircraft came down in the local area. Although not a comprehensive list, some of these are:

1. A North American Mustang single-seater fighter crashed in the Devil's Punchbowl in 1943, whilst trying to reach the nearby airfield at Dunsfold. The pilot bailed out and was unharmed. The crashed aircraft was duly inspected by local children, and it seems that various souvenirs were taken away at the time.

North American Mustang

2. In the summer of 1944, Jane Durham and her mother watched from their house at the edge of Ludshott Common as a Douglas C.47 Dakota transport plane made a controlled crash landing on a flat part of the Common, behind their house. It was apparently on its way back from supplying the troops in France after the Normandy D-Day landings, but experienced engine trouble, and landed on a flat section of the common known as Timber Way, possibly mistaking it for a temporary airfield. The two ladies rushed to the scene, armed only with a garden rake (in case of fire), and met the two crew members, who were apparently shaken but unharmed by their ordeal. She does not know what became of the aircraft after that day, but it was probably dismantled and taken away.

Douglas C-47 Dakota

3. On the night of 21st January 1944, a Heinkel 177 four-engined bomber, registration F8+HH flew in a formation from a base in France, intending to bombard a collection of ships that had assembled on the Thames in London, being prepared for use in the forthcoming Normandy landings. The aircraft was spotted by a de Havilland Mosquito night fighter, on a navigational exercise, the German bomber having been caught in a cone of searchlights at the time. Closing the range, the Mosquito

Heinkel 177

pilot asked for the searchlights to be turned off, so that the target's aircrew would not spot them. When they were within 1,000 feet, the Mosquito opened fire, causing a violent explosion on the bomber's port wing. The Heinkel caught fire, and plunged into a steep spiral dive. It crash-landed at Windy Gap, between Churt and Grayshott. Three of the crew baled out, and were taken prisoner, but the pilot and two others stayed on board. Two of those perished, but the tail gunner survived the crash.

Curtis C-46 Commando

4. On the 30th June 1944, at exactly 9.10am, a V-1 "doodlebug" flying bomb came down and crashed in grounds formerly part of the "Land of Nod". It had been launched from a site near the coast of northern France and, with a warhead of 1,870lbs of high explosive, it had flown at a speed of 400 miles per hour for just under fifteen minutes before the motor cut out and it dived to the ground. Apparently, it caused a very loud explosion, but with little actual damage and no injuries were caused. A large hole in the ground was there for a several months after.

5. On 6th May 1945, just two days before VE (Victory in Europe) Day, a twin-engine American Curtis Commander hospital transport aircraft crashed into one of the four military radio masts on Gibbet Hill, at the spot where the National Trust café now stands. The mast was totally demolished and thirty-two people died in the crash, in what was, at the time, the worst air disaster in UK aviation history. Despite this, little was reported of the disaster at the time, as the country was engulfed in the euphoria of peace, after six long years of war. The tragedy of the accident, however, was that all of the passengers were wounded military personnel, most of whom were stretcher cases, and they were literally within minutes of returning to land in England and safety.

Members of the Whitaker family examine the V-1 bomb crater.
Note parts of the Doodlebug engine lying to the left.

CHURCH WEDDINGS

Throughout the war years, St. Luke's and other local churches continued to be a magnet for the celebration of marriage, although the records show that the weddings that were celebrated had a pronounced military emphasis during this time, possibly not surprisingly.

In this period, a total of fifty-five weddings were celebrated at St. Luke's, and these numbers included thirty serving soldiers, another eight from the Royal Air Force, and also four Navy personnel. Amongst the brides at church were three munitions workers, two members of the Women's Auxiliary Air Force, two RAF cooks, one VAD nurse, and one Land Army girl.

And it is not surprising to see that the Canadians were also well represented among the grooms at church. There were a total of eleven marriages at St. Luke's in this period between Canadian soldiers from the camps in the area and girls from Grayshott and nearby. Presumably this resulted in a minor exodus to the New World after the war, as these local girls embarked on their new lives in a strange, but welcoming, country.

In the whole of the United Kingdom, during the period 1939 to 1946, a total of 44,886 Canadian service men married British women, and the vast majority lived their married lives across the Atlantic Ocean.

A 1940 wartime wedding

THE END

The end of the war in Europe was on Victory in Europe (VE) Day, the 8th May 1945, which was a Tuesday. To mark the occasion, Grayshott School was closed for two days, to enable the children to take part in the celebrations. Grayshott joined with the whole country in rejoicing at the end of six years of hostility and austerity. A special service of thanks was conducted by Canon Ottley at St. Luke's, and the Village Hall hosted a noisy and exuberant celebration dance, which was heavily attended.

The following Monday, the 14th May, the school was closed early in the afternoon, and the children were marched the one mile in single file down to Amesbury School in Hindhead in order to greet Field Marshall Bernard Montgomery who was visiting the school. His son had been a pupil there in 1936, and he himself had used part of the school buildings as a rear base to nearby Portsmouth when finalising the plans for the D Day landings, the previous year, in 1944.

Ten days later, on Empire Day, the 24th May, the school celebrated the special occasion with a full programme of national songs and inspiring talks. A flagpole was presented to the school by a Major Reynolds, and a flag by a Mrs Harris. The school was closed for the afternoon, the delighted children being treated to a half day holiday.

Throughout the six long years of war, the people of Grayshott did what they could to help with the national effort. New allotments were opened up for the cultivation of food crops, extra land was found for air raid trenches, there was food storage in the Village Hall, and requisition of iron railings for melting down for munitions took place, amongst many other examples.

It should also be noted that a great deal of clothes-making took place in the village, to keep the troops duly supplied. The figures show that a total of 10,261 garments were made for this purpose during the war period. This included 867 jerseys, 2,392 pairs of socks, 664 overcoats in oiled wool, all of which were sent to the Royal Air Force, the Royal Artillery, the Royal and Merchant Navies and the Women's Auxiliary Air Force.

In national efforts, also, the village did well. In War Savings Week in 1941 a total of £4,856 was raised, for Warship Week in 1942 the amount of £8,527, and in Salute for Soldiers Week in 1945 the sum of £47,177 was freely given, jointly raised with neighbouring villages.

In 1945, with the war in Europe over, the Grayshott Women's Institute spent much of the year busily knitting garments which were then sent overseas for the children of the ravaged countries of liberated Europe, at a time of great suffering for the survivors of the war and their families.

The Village had played its part.

THE WAR MEMORIAL

After the end of the war, it was decided to alter the village War Memorial. A new plinth was added to the base, in order to accommodate the names of nineteen service personnel, amongst those others who perished in the conflict. The names are:

Beard RG	Chegwyn DA	Cornish GF
Edwards GE	Edwards RJ	Gilling-Lax GG
Holme-Sumner BD	Hopkins-Cox T	Harris FG
Lovett AS	Madgwick EW	Moore G
Murphy CA	Oatley GR	Parham DAR
Roberts DMK	Snelling EA	Wade PA
Wade RTC		

At the back of St. Luke's Church, there is an illuminated plaque with a Roll of Honour. It shows the names of a total of two hundred and fifty-three men and women of Grayshott who served during the conflict, together with those who made the supreme sacrifice.

CHAPTER EIGHT

FROM THEN TO NOW – a modern village

The end of the Second World War found a Britain that was exhausted, militarily and economically, but with its reputation enhanced on the world stage, with its unique role in helping to gain the Allied victory. But it came at a cost, with the continued restrictions imposed by rationing, and with the need to repair the extensive damage caused by enemy actions in all major cities, as well as the search for employment of hundreds and thousands of military personnel, returning to their families and to civilian life.

Situated away from any major city centres, Grayshott was probably fortunate in suffering little physical damage during the conflict. Bomb damage was relatively slight, and the same can be said of civilian casualties. The major effect of the war years came in the form of the many thousands of military personnel stationed in the area, most of whom were made welcome by the inhabitants of Grayshott. The Army was now gone, and the village had adjusted easily to the vacuum caused by its departure.

Having said thus, the military did leave its mark, in the shape of damaged roads and pathways, to say nothing of the extensive environmental upheaval caused to the commons and open spaces surrounding the area. The National Trust laboured for many years to bring back such areas as Ludshott Common to their natural states, encouraging the return of local wildlife with the re-introduction of foliage and ground cover. This was to take years of careful repair work and management to resolve.

In the years that have passed since the end of the Second World War, Grayshott has seen significant changes and development, both socially as well as to the fabric of the village. New estates have been built, smaller housing developments and infilling have all taken place, and there has been the ever-present challenge shown by the conflict between the pressure of growth and the desire to maintain a village atmosphere. In general terms, Grayshott has been successful in achieving these supposedly conflicting goals.

The major housing developments that have taken place to date are the Kingswood Firs Estate that was being developed in the 1950s and 60s, and the Waggoners Estate, that grew on the old Searchlight Field in the 1960s and beyond. To these must now be added the new development of land adjacent to Applegarth Farm Shop on the Headley Road, known as Applegarth Vale.

Immediately after the War, the local Council foresaw the need for an expansion of housing, with a growth in the population as well as the urgency of rehousing families who, for various reasons, were without a permanent home.

In what was seen as a short-term measure, the now vacated collection of military buildings which were located at what was called Camp Superior on Ludshott Common, originally constructed in 1941, was given over to what would these days be called Social Housing. Prior to that, at the end of the War, the camp was used to house Canadian soldiers returning from the conflict in Europe and beyond, who were waiting anxiously to go back to their home country.

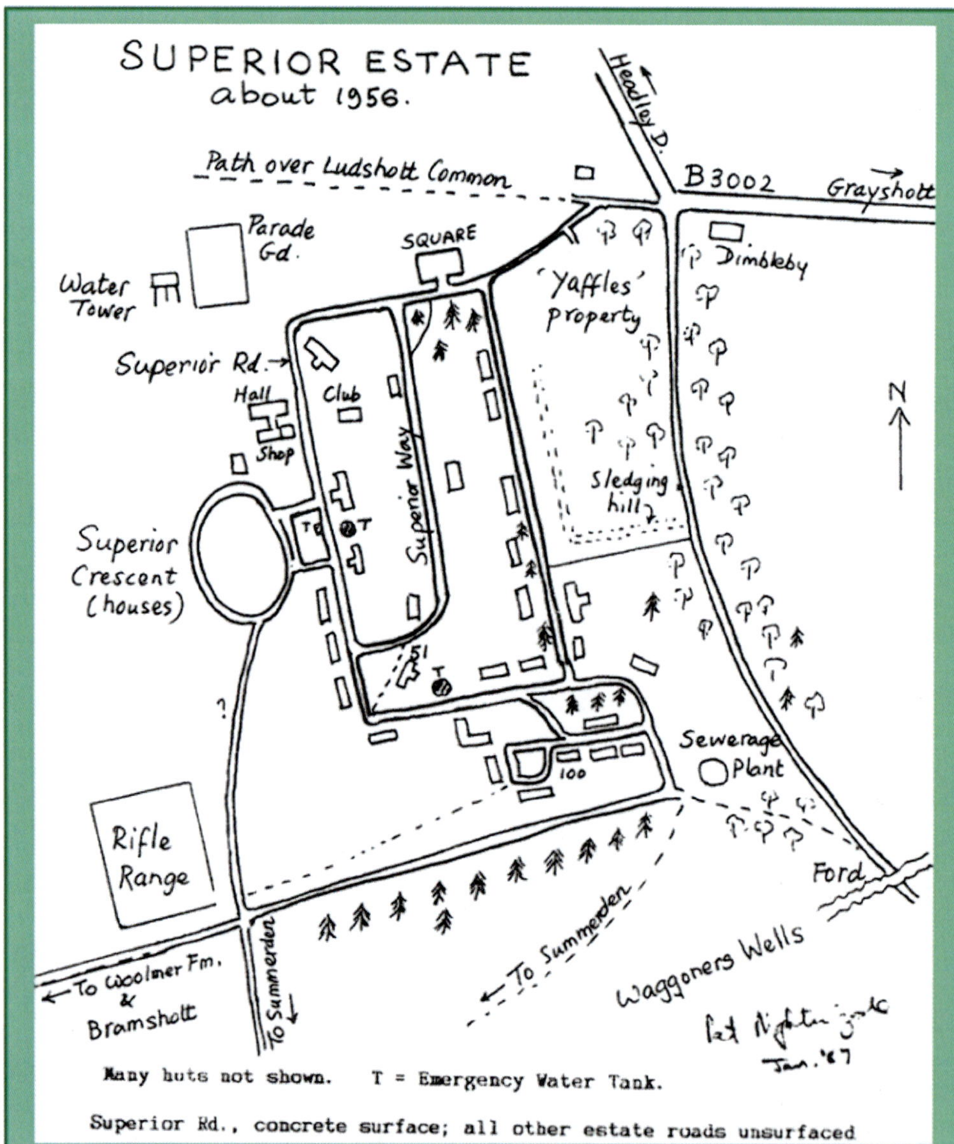

Superior Camp estates around 1956, as remembered by a resident

The camp was finally vacated in 1946, and, as soon as this happened, Petersfield Rural District Council requisitioned the site, converting the army huts into 146 housing units, which were capable of providing a home to some 650 or so people. A shop was also provided at the same time.

The site was renamed "Superior Estate", but was still known by everyone locally as "The Camp". It gained a rough and ready reputation, as a number of its inhabitants were sometimes known to the police, and a large number of them were without regular jobs. But many families maintained happy memories of The Camp, and children gained their formative years there, despite the pressure of increased numbers placed upon Grayshott School, which coped with resilience.

It was not until 1962 that The Camp was finally vacated, when all the tenants had been rehoused. At that time, all the buildings were demolished and the site reverted to the landowners, the National Trust. Today, as you walk down the remaining concrete tracks, you can still see the outline of many of the buildings through the trees and undergrowth, as the ghosts of the past cast their shadows on the present.

Looking at other previously used military facilities, the local council also considered using the solid buildings forming part of the old searchlight unit off Headley Road, already being used temporarily by a local family, but nothing came of this, as the buildings were considered to be unsuitable for long-term residential use. After this, in 1947, a total of sixteen new houses were built nearby, in Beech Lane, and other sites were also considered at the same time.

KINGSWOOD FIRS

In the latter part of the 1950s what is now the Kingswood Firs estate was being developed. Historically it is believed that this area of land could well have been a royal plantation going back to early Tudor times.

The development consisted of a total of eighty building plots, featuring architecturally-designed houses with large gardens, all of which were laid out on an attractive low density suburban basis, retaining as much of the existing shrubbery and tree numbers as could be contained within the development, with open spaces and an efficient system of road lighting.

It was seen to be mostly attractive to commuters with growing families as well as retired persons. At the time, the developers restricted the building work to the higher ground between Kingswood Lane and Stoney Bottom, and did not encroach on the lower levels, so keeping the estate very largely as a self-contained unit, without bordering directly onto the village itself.

Kingswood Firs today

Waggoners estate today

WAGGONERS

At the other end of Grayshott, on its western borders, planning permission was given in the late 1960s for the other large development, when the old Searchlight Field became what is now known as Waggoners Estate. Permission was given for the construction of one hundred and three houses on these fields, and it is today characterised by a general feeling of space, with low density housing of varied designs and styles, being served by gently curving roadways with wide verges, and many trees.

At the time, it was feared by many local inhabitants that these two large developments would seriously undermine the nature of the village, which up to then had been a somewhat private local community, possibly inward looking in the most benevolent fashion, but now learning to accept the presence of several hundred more people, largely arriving from outside the immediate area. It was felt that integration would prove difficult, as many of the newer residents were commuters or retired folk, to a large extent coming from outside the area. In the end, though, these fears proved ill-founded, and Grayshott has seen the benefits of having a larger and more diverse community, with a strengthening of social activities and local affairs generally.

APPLEGARTH VALE

Close by to Waggoners we see the creation and development of a new estate of houses that is taking place. Consisting of a mixed development of three- and four-bedroomed houses, plus a required proportion of social housing, Applegarth Vale is taking shape on what was previously a green and open area that had seen agricultural use in years gone by. As the new community emerges, the hope is that it will, over time, become immersed into the social fabric of Grayshott, and that the village will grow and prosper with the benefit of this addition to the area.

TUDOR HOUSE and TUDOR CLOSE

Tudor Close, with its twenty-six houses, is situated off Kingswood Firs, and sits on the site of the old Zachary Merton Convalescent Home.

Mr Zachary Merton (1843-1915) was a member of a wealthy family of Anglo-German industrialists and philanthropists, and was a partner in the successful London metal trading company known as Henry R Merton & Company. Over the years the company developed world-wide interests, and became a major player in the growth of industrial Britain. After the end of the First World War, the company was later reorganised and ultimately became the British Metal Corporation.

Zachary Merton was of a most selfless and charitable nature, and he spent both considerable energies as well as sums of money in helping the poor children of London and elsewhere. Despite being married twice, he had no children of his own, but he provided generously for the education of his step children, as well as many others, of all ages and calling.

At one point, in his later years, he was admitted to the Middlesex Hospital in London for a serious operation. He, with a fellow patient, vowed that if they survived the operations, they would establish six hospitals. Mr Merton would build them and the other patient would provide the furnishings and contents. The operations on both patients were successful but sadly the other patient reneged on the promise that he had made. However, on his death in 1915, Merton left the then considerable sum of £350,000 in his will for the establishment of a trust to be used for charitable purposes after his death, which enabled the building of convalescent homes, and many small hospitals bearing his name.

The hospitals that were built included one in Grayshott, the area being known for its clean air and healthy surroundings, and this was built in about nine acres of land in 1936 in a well-wooded and inconspicuous site close to the old A3 London to Portsmouth trunk road.

Tudor House, consisting at the time of a central block with a clock tower and three projecting wings, was a substantial construction, and it served its purpose throughout the war years and beyond. In later years it became a successful Nursing Home, and even acted as a sometime overspill for Grayshott School.

After closure, however, the building was finally demolished in the 1970s, and the site was developed into what is now Tudor Close, forming a pleasing residential backwater to the village.

Zachary Merton Convalescent Home,
now the site of Tudor Close

THE GRAYSHOTT AND DISTRICT HOUSING ASSOCIATION

The Grayshott and District Housing Association has for many years been a long and successful part of the life of the village.

The Association started life back in 1935, with Mrs Charlotte Lyndon, the Wife of Doctor Arnold Lyndon (both of whom we met earlier) being the initial driving force and its first Chairman. Her long-term vision was to help to support and maintain a true rural community, but it was to the great loss of the village as well as the Association that she sadly died only a year after the foundation of the Association.

Its remit at the time was, and still remains, to seek to provide good and substantial housing for persons with a connection with the village (either through family or work) at affordable prices, with rents that are lower than the normal market rate.

The first properties were at 1-6 Beech Lane and 1-6 Northwood Cottages, purchased in the latter part of 1936, after they had both come onto the open market. Thereafter, the Association built up its portfolio over the years, with the acquisition of properties in varying parts of the village, in many cases requiring renovation, repair and upgrading, as might prove necessary.

The Association is now in the enviable position of being the owner of a total of thirty-one properties in Grayshott, varying from one-bedroomed flats to two and three-bedroomed houses, all managed and maintained locally, and for the benefit and well being of members of the local community.

There are many people in Grayshott for whom the Association is largely an unknown quantity. It operates quietly and without fuss in the background of the everyday life of the village, but nonetheless has shown over the years that it acts as one of the powerful forces that help to provide social cohesion to the community.

It has further plans for expansion, which will be to the benefit of many who wish to anchor their roots within the village in the decades to come.

The Village & St Luke's

The Square in the Village

THE GRAYSHOTT CLINIC AND A TIME CAPSULE

As we saw earlier, the Clinic at Grayshott, constructed after the Great War at the junction of School Road and Beech Hanger Road, was eventually sold for redevelopment. The demolition gave the unique opportunity for the Time Capsule built into the foundation stone to be opened and the contents examined.

This revealed a collection of coins dated 1920 wrapped in leather with a wax seal which had subsequently disintegrated.

Also, a canvas roll was found to contain a copy of the Times newspaper for Wednesday the 27th October 1920 along with a supplement to the Times dated Monday the 11th October 1920 for the "Welcome Home to our Ambassador Prince".

Following the discovery, the contents were replaced in 2011, together with similar items from the present day into a display plinth on the corner of School Road and Headley Road, where it can be seen today, for the interest of passers-by.

The Grayshott Clinic foundation stone

We must also mention the developments that took place in this period to the north east of the village, consisting in what is now Rozeldene (with twenty-two houses), Forest Dale, (fifteen), and The Moorings (thirty-one houses plus sixteen apartments). It is quite accepted that these fall outside the boundaries of Grayshott village itself, being actually part of Hindhead in Surrey. Having said thus, all of these houses and flats are to the south of what was the old A3 Portsmouth road, and in many ways are seen to form an extension to the village. Many people consider that the geographic limits of Grayshott should be extended to include these areas, and certainly a large number of the residents there consider themselves part of the Grayshott community. There are many conflicting issues at stake, however, and this is surely a matter that will need to be addressed by others in the future.

Grayshott in the snow – 2010

COMMERCIAL LIFE

The 1950s onwards have shown a growth in the commercial and business life of the village, in order to satisfy the needs of a population of over two thousand residents. The two major village roads, namely Headley Road and Crossways Road, are both host to a good number of shops and offices, with retail units, restaurants, supermarkets, offices, hair and beauty salons, estate agents, and others, including the inevitable charity shops, and the village pub, all of which have their own part to play in the daily life of the village. Headley Road itself boasts a total in excess of sixty units, and Crossways Road over twenty. We must also include those outside the immediate village, such as Applegarth Farm Shop, Grayshott Health Spa, both on the road to Headley, and also the Pottery in School Road, the latter being a well known and successful pottery business, trading since the mid 1960s.

It is inevitable that there will be changes over the years, as demands vary and shopping and retail trends alter. Until the 1980s, for example, there were three garages in the village, the largest of which was owned and run by Mr Hersey on the site where is now the Phyllis Tuckwell charity shop, Light Lines and Business Connections.

The village square in Headley Road was built in the late 1960s as a shopping precinct surrounded by two-storey buildings, and it quickly became a popular focal point in the heart of the village. Later on, in 2010, it was completely refurbished, with the laying of a new surface, and the provision of seating as well as the planting of a number of trees. Today it is the venue for a variety of social and other gatherings throughout the year as well as being home for a number of shops and other businesses.

Each year, a magnificent Christmas tree is erected in the square as part of the seasonal celebrations, with hundreds of lights and streamers, and playing host to the annual carol service on Christmas Eve, which is always attended by large crowds.

As well as the tree, for many years Grayshott has put on a Christmas lights display that must be without parallel. Tens of thousands of tiny light bulbs glittering beautifully throughout the many trees in the centre of the village have caused people each year to travel from literally miles around to view the display. The stunning show has long become a welcome annual fixture in the village.

Grayshott Garage, then, after and now

Crossways Road and St Luke's

THE MURAL IN THE SQUARE

The official opening of the refurbished square in 2010 was the moment when a specially commissioned mural of tiles was unveiled there. Commissioned by Grayshott Pottery, the mural recorded the breadth of the flourishing groups and associations in the village. Each highly-coloured individual stoneware tile took on average three hours to design and hand-decorate, with a total of forty-six organisations or groups being interpreted by the Pottery's artists, before each tile was fired at 1,250 degrees centigrade.

The whole unique project was managed by Phil Bates, the Trustee of the Pottery, and its Production director Glenn Myers, and took some eleven months to complete. Today it forms a fascinating backdrop when walking round the square.

Mural in The Square

Blue plaque in The Square

It is possibly surprising that the village centre of Grayshott continues to flourish, in view of the challenges and threats with which it finds itself faced, as do all shopping centres that exist to serve the needs of the local community. The magnetic draw of out-of-town supermarkets, to say nothing of the growing influence of on-line shopping, all leave their mark on the prosperity of local shops, as the buying habits of the general public change over the years.

On top of this, it could be argued that Grayshott is in fact a victim of its own success, the frequent congestion of traffic in the village centre, as shoppers find it increasingly difficult to find somewhere to park bears witness.

The growth of traffic has been a concern for many years now. As far back as October 1947 a proposal was put by the Police to the local Council to build a car park in the village. In this particular case, the plan was to build a car park on part of the village green at the junction of Headley Road and Whitmore Vale Road, but this proposal was dropped following a strong petition signed by over three hundred and fifty people.

In the end, 1970 saw the construction of the car park that is adjacent to the Fox & Pelican garden, behind the estate offices of Peter Leete and Partners. Since then, there have been two further car parks built in the village, one constructed in 1979 in Crossways Road, on the old site formerly owned by Chapman, Lowry and Puttick Ltd, well known local Builders, Contractors & Decorators, and the other in Glen Road, which came into use in 1988.

All three car parks have the attraction of being free of charge. As early as 1975 there was a suggestion of charging for car parking, but the Parish Council has always strongly opposed this, on the basis that one of the attractions of Grayshott as a shopping centre is free on-street and off-street parking.

However, the large amount of traffic passing through the village, some stopping and some not, continues to be a problem, one for which there seem to be few solutions, on top of occasional speeding vehicles and inconsiderate parking.

The question of speeding is by no means new, as the problem goes all the way back to 1912, when a case of speeding and dangerous driving was first encountered. A Mr Edwin Slade of Shaftesbury Avenue in London was prosecuted for driving through the village at 26 miles an hour. His plea that there was a deliberate speed trap met with the response that even at only half that speed he would still have been over the statutory speed limit. He was fined £1.00 with 12 shillings (60p) costs.

It is now the case that all roads within the parish are subject to some form of speed limit or other, with traffic calming and speed bumps located at various points.

In order to promote the village to a wider audience, The Buy in Grayshott group (BIG) had been formed in 1997. For many years this took an active lead in promoting the idea of encouraging shopping in the village, organising such things as the village Christmas lights and also the Grayshott in Bloom annual hanging baskets scheme. Sadly, after nearly twenty years, it was felt that the scheme had run its course, and it was quietly disbanded, with the hopes that other schemes might follow.

Despite the various pressures, the village continues to serve the needs of its local population, and has managed to survive, even thrive, in the face of a mixture of competitive threats and burgeoning problems that are possibly inevitable in any local, reasonably prosperous community.

THE VILLAGE IS REWARDED

Within the last few years, Grayshott has received many national as well as local awards, due to the enthusiasm and hard work shown by many members of the community in promoting the well being and prosperity of the village.

In the years 2002 and 2005 Grayshott competed against a large number of villages in the county, and was successful in being proclaimed Hampshire Village of the Year.

If that was not enough, in 2002 it was also the first village to win the special prestigious award of the Business Village of the Year for Southern and South East England in the face of stiff competition.

In that same year as well, HRH The Prince of Wales launched a special "Business in the Community" award for the overall winner of the business category in the Calor Village of the Year competition, which was keenly contested by over 1,500 villages throughout England and Wales. The award was intended to recognise the importance of rural businesses to the fabric of village life. The judges clearly recognised the interactive role between business and the community in Grayshott.

Participants were invited to a ceremony in London, where the representatives from Grayshott, Dick Smith, Phil Bates and Peter Hatch were elated to discover that Grayshott had won the ultimate business award. They were greatly honoured to receive the winner's plaque from HRH The Princess Royal on behalf of the village.

Other awards to the village in recent years include

- 2005 Best Village award for Business in the Community, South England.
- 2007 East Hampshire Village of the Year.
- 2008 Best Business in the Community Award.
- 2010 Hampshire Village of the Year runner up.
- 2011 Business and the Community Together Award.
- 2014 Regeneration & Improvement of Community Facilities and Infrastructure Award.

2002 Business Award with HRH Princess Anne

Village of the Year Winners, 2002 & 2005

As if these accolades were not enough, the year 2016 saw the village crowned Champion of Champions by the Hampshire Association of Local Councils under its awards scheme, a recognition only given in exceptional circumstances, at the same time as being honoured with a raft of seven other awards.

There seems little doubt that Grayshott continues to thrive commercially, and that the community will carry on reaping the benefits as a result.

THE POTTERY AT GRAYSHOTT

The village can justifiably boast of being home to one of Southern England's few remaining working commercial potteries. Sitting prominently on the side of the valley that leads down to Whitmore Vale, the Pottery has become a firmly established local industry since its birth in 1956, and its success is such that it is now the largest pottery in the South of England.

It emerged from the old Kingswood Pottery in Brook, having connections with Compton Pottery which was originally started by Mary Watts, the wife of the great Victorian painter, G F Watts. Later it acquired the business of Dartington Pottery in 2005, enabling it to transfer a new set of skills using specialised glazing techniques to achieve stunning vibrant hand-painted finishes.

Today, it produces an exclusive range of studio art ceramics for galleries and homes around the UK, including bespoke ceramics for well-known celebrity chefs as well as catering-ware for many national high street pubs and restaurants.

It ranks as a valuable asset of the village, and its popularity is enhanced by a veritable Aladdin's Cave of a gift shop in addition to a well-run cafeteria and coffee shop.

Grayshott Pottery

GRAYSHOTT PARISH COUNCIL

The Parish Council, which looks after the interests of the businesses and population of the village, has been in active existence since 1902. Its role is to represent the civil parish without any political bias or prejudice as well as looking after its assets and fostering community spirit.

Its ten Councillors meet regularly in the Nancy Littlejohn Room at the Village Hall where, generally speaking, all meetings are open to the public and to the press.

The Council owns a large number of assets on behalf of the Grayshott community, including The Village Square, Lyndon Green, the War Memorial and garden, the Village Green, Recreation Ground and Pavilion, skate park and tennis courts, to name but some.

The Council forms an intrinsic and important part of the life of the village. It is happy to take an active and approachable role in decision making, for the benefit of the community, and is regarded as having an essential role in promoting the well being and prosperity of the village as a whole.

THE MILLENNIUM SIGN, AND A PIG PARTY, 2000

During early 1997, the question arose as to how the village was to commemorate and celebrate the coming of the new millennium in 2000. There was a great deal of discussion, and committees were formed in order to gain ideas, and then turn them into reality.

The Millennium Sculpture

The idea of the Millennium sign took hold in early 1999, based on an initial design by local resident Pam McNichol. It was also decided to organise a large party and carnival in the village to celebrate the event.

The sign took the form of a circular metal column, completed in bronze and stainless steel, with a top logo design showing outline images of St. Luke's Church, the Fox & Pelican pub, as well as designs of local trees. The eventual height of the column itself was approximately 7ft 6ins (2285mm), and it was set in the ground within a bronze base of 4ft 6ins (1371mm) diameter bearing the design of the sun, under which was a time capsule, placed there by the local Brownies and Beavers.

The main work was undertaken and supervised by the Haslemere Forge Ltd, and was completed in time for its formal unveiling on mid-summer's day, June 24th, 2000.

On that same day, the village celebrated with a lively carnival, with a Carnival Queen and a parade of fifteen floats processing gaily and noisily through the village. These included a poppy-decorated Reliant Robin from the British Legion, a Star Wars float and an Old MacDonald's Farm float decorated by the Grayshott Babes and Toddlers. Also taking part were the Hayling Island marching band and the Liphook Majorettes.

It was estimated that upwards of five thousand people attended the celebrations throughout the day, with the Party in Grayshott (PIG) centred around Lyndon Green going on until the late hours of the evening. It was said at the time that the village had not seen such a party since the end of the war celebrations in 1945.

The whole event was rated a huge success – Grayshott had enjoyed itself in style.

GRAYSHOTT ENJOYS A SOCIAL LIFE

The social life of the village has continued to grow and prosper over the years, as is shown by the many clubs, societies and village groups that we see.

Grayshott Social Club, tucked away down Hill Road, has been one of the social hubs of the village now for more than a hundred years, providing facilities and entertainment for over five hundred of its members. Its bar and function rooms provide a full programme of musical entertainment, games and sport, and in 2016 the club's "community" status was recognised by the Parish Council and the club building and its lands added to the list of Grayshott Community Assets.

The Fox & Pelican public house has been a social centre of the village since before the end of the 19th Century, and continues to offer a friendly venue where one can enjoy a meal and drink with family and friends, as well as a large beer garden and children's play area.

There is also a good choice of restaurants, offering traditional English as well as Nepalese, Turkish and Indian cuisine. The range may be thought surprising, given the size of the village, but they are popular, and satisfy a strong local demand, as well as drawing in customers from outlying towns and villages.

St. Luke's Church is set in the heart of the village, and is the host to a number of nationally regarded classical concerts each year, with first class performances, and participation by famous

Fun in the Village Hall

A Concert in St Luke's – Vivaldi's Gloria in 2008

artistes and composers, such as Sir Karl Jenkins, CBE. The reputation of "Grayshott Concerts" continues to flourish, under the watchful care of its organisers.

There are too many clubs and organisations to mention individually (over eighteen at the last count, and rising!), but, as examples, we see the Grayshott Gardeners, which holds many events throughout the year, with monthly meetings, many with invited speakers, as well as horticultural displays and competitions, which are keenly supported.

The Grayshott Stagers, in its present form, goes back to February 1951, with their many well organised productions and musicals, including Treasure Island, shown here, in 2006. Today, the Society caters for a broad range of interests spread over a wide age range. In addition, all other forms of stagecraft can be practised, such as costume design and manufacture, scenery design, lighting etc.

The 1st Grayshott Scouts with cubs and beavers celebrated their centenary in 2007, and there are numerous other memberships that do much to protect and promote the village itself.

The Grayshott Society was formed when three villagers banded together in order to try to protect and enhance the traditional side of Grayshott life, by encouraging the interest and support of residents and others in such areas as planning and associated matters. It continues to play an active role in village life, specifically in relation to local buildings, the natural environment and the preservation of the "character" of Grayshott.

Grayshott Heritage, originally called the Grayshott Village Archive, has at its objective the preservation and promotion of Grayshott's history, for interest, reflection, discussion and study. It has an active website, which provides an interesting and informative window onto the story of the development and growth of the village.

The Village Hall remains the venue for a full and varied selection of activities. As well as fulfilling the needs of local groups for a home for their interests, it has also provided platforms for both local and national political events, and also well-known radio shows.

In February 1954, for example, the Hall hosted an episode of "Twenty Questions" and also "What's My Line?", with Richard Dimbleby and other famous names, in aid of the Roof Repair Fund. The event was a sell-out.

Stretching throughout the whole village, the Hidden Gardens of Grayshott scheme provides a unique insight into the private gardens of the village. Every two years, in Spring, a large number of houses open their gardens to public viewing, and this popular event sees many hundreds of people visiting gardens of different shapes and sizes, including the two village allotment sites. Some gardens are large and palatial, some are small and quirky, but all offer ideas and inspiration to their visitors.

Grayshott Gardens

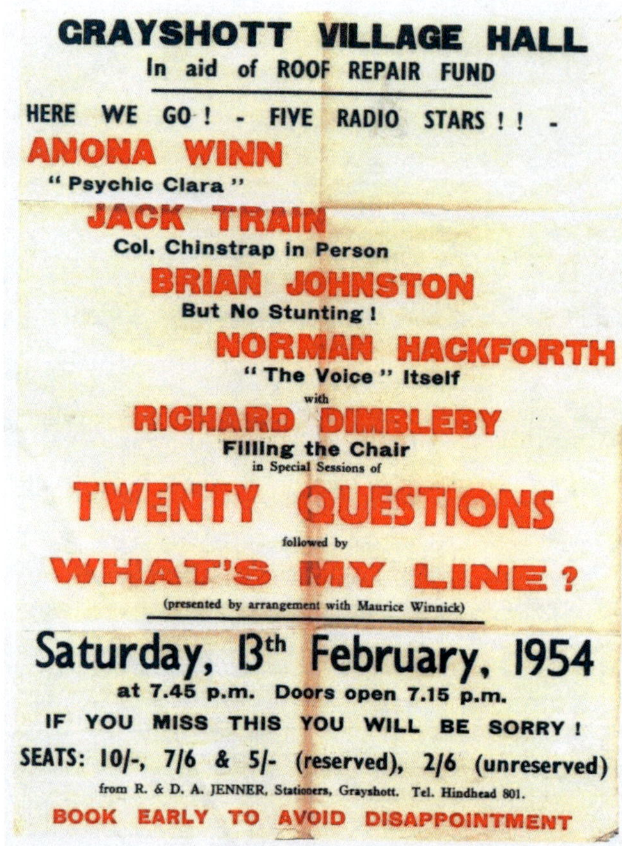

An Evening in Grayshott Village Hall 1954

"What's My Line?" 1954

The popular and extensive playing fields on the road to Headley are home to the Grayshott Cricket and Football clubs, with a fine clubhouse, together with a second children's play area as well as cricket nets and a skate park. There is also a thriving Croquet Club, which gets together on the outfield of the cricket pitch during the summer months, catering for both beginners as well as experienced players, the Grayshott Tennis Club, which is always open to new members, and Indoor Bowls, which meets in the Village Hall during the winter months.

And further down the road there is the Grayshott Health Spa, set in its own 47 acres of grounds and gardens, and adjoining over 700 acres of stunning National Trust land. It has come a long way since the days of Edward I'Anson in the 19th century, but today it boasts a world class reputation for its health regimes, and is undoubtedly a tangible asset to the village.

And now …

It is difficult to appreciate that, a little over one hundred and fifty years ago, Grayshott simply did not exist as a village in its own right. It is worth recalling that, where it lies now was, until recent historic times, nothing more than wild countryside, with harsh vegetation and inhospitable scrubland, which managed to support just a handful of families on a bare subsistence level. The farming land, then called Grayshotte (and various other earlier names) was to be found down the road towards Headley, and that itself was the extent of the community for many generations.

Change came in the early and middle years of the 19th Century, as we have seen, due to the various influences in play at the time, and these may be said to have pretty well "kickstarted" the birth of the village as we know it today. Grayshott grew as a community that served and provisioned the needs of the larger houses that came into being, as the reputation of Hindhead and the surrounding areas blossomed. The establishment of the railway network put the whole area within easy reach of London, and the popularity flowing from the reputation of "Little Switzerland" gave impetus to the development of shops and the growth of houses in the village.

Since then, Grayshott has seen significant growth over the years, with the establishment of large residential estates, such as Kingswood Firs, and Waggoners Field as well as much local infilling such as to be found in places like Beech Lane and Crossways Road. There have also been a number of apartment buildings constructed, to satisfy the needs of not only an ageing population, but also for more affordable housing.

The village has developed and maintained an enviable local identity, although it obviously suffers from the pressures of a population that is more mobile than in years past, with a majority no longer working in the direct neighbourhood, but commuting every day to nearby towns as well as London itself. But despite this, there has, for many years, been a solid core of local families, going back a number of generations, that has helped to give roots to the village, and to provide a sense of permanence to the community that has grown and prospered over the years. It is perhaps this idea of continuity, in the face of all the shifts and influences in society today, that is the greatest appeal that Grayshott offers, in the sense that despite all the rigours of modern life, Grayshott can offer these deep roots, and sense of permanence, that makes it a little bit special today.

This makes it a true English village in all senses.

BIBLIOGRAPHY and SOURCES

Dame Agnes Weston, "My Life among the Blue Jackets"; James Nesbit & Company, 1914.

J H Smith, "Grayshott, the story of a Hampshire Village"; John Owen Smith, 2002.

Thomas Wright, "Hindhead, or the English Switzerland"; Simpkin, Marshall & Company, 1898.

John Owen Smith, "All Tanked Up", 1994 & 2008.

Bramshott & Liphook Preservation Society, "Liphook, Bramshott, and the Canadians; B&LPS.

John Owen Smith, "On the Trail of Flora Thompson", 1997.

The Author, "Grayshott's War Memorial, 1914 to 1982", Noyant Publications, 2014.

N. Best, "The Greatest Day in History", 2008.

Bob Ogley, "Surrey at War" 1939-1945.

Surrey History Centre, Woking, Surrey. `

Farnham Museum.

Farnham Herald, 1914 issues.

The Grayshott Magazine, issues 1898 to 1935.

US Army Air Force, aircraft accident records.

With grateful thanks, to the following, for their welcome contributions and assistance:–

Mr Tony Cunningham.

Grayshott Heritage.

Mr Phil Bates.

Mrs Jane Durham.

Major Jeremy Whitaker.

Mr Andrew Hall.

Mr Trevor Baxter.

Mrs Briony Johnson.

"Fromtheairdrones", and Mr John Senior.

Made in United States
North Haven, CT
27 August 2024

56616774R00077